W9-BNT-703

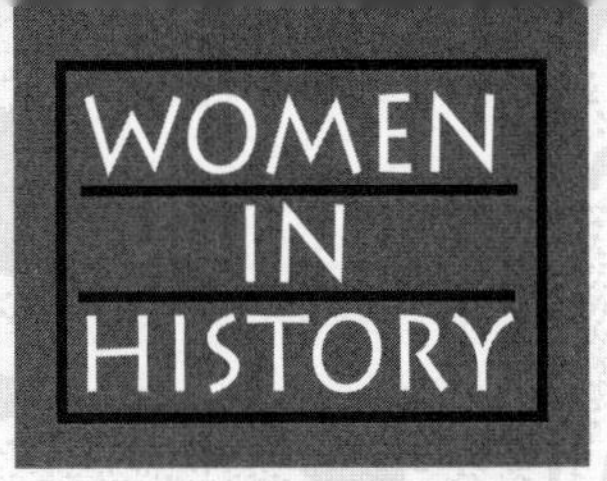

Women of Ancient Egypt

Anne Wallace Sharp

LUCENT BOOKS
An imprint of Thomson Gale, a part of The Thomson Corporation

MEMORIAL SCHOOL LIBRARY
81 C[illegible]
HULL, MASSACHUSETTS 02045

THOMSON
GALE™

Detroit • New York • San Francisco • San Diego • New Haven, Conn. • Waterville, Maine • London • Munich

© 2005 Thomson Gale, a part of The Thomson Corporation.

Thomson and Star Logo are trademarks and Gale and Lucent Books are registered trademarks used herein under license.

For more information, contact
Lucent Books
27500 Drake Rd.
Farmington Hills, MI 48331–3535
Or you can visit our Internet site at http://www.gale.com

ALL RIGHTS RESERVED.
No part of this work covered by the copyright hereon may be reproduced or used in any form or by any means—graphic, electronic, or mechanical, including photocopying, recording, taping, Web distribution, or information storage retrieval systems—without the written permission of the publisher.

Every effort has been made to trace the owners of copyrighted material.

LIBRARY OF CONGRESS CATALOGING–IN–PUBLICATION DATA

Sharp, Anne Wallace.
Women of Ancient Egypt / by Anne Wallace Sharp.
p. cm. — (Women in history)
Includes bibliographical references and index.
ISBN 1–59018–361–4 (hardcover : alk. paper)
1. Women—Egypt—History, Ancient—Juvenile literature. 2. Egypt—Social life and customs—To 332 B.C.—Juvenile literature. 3. Egypt—Civilization—To 332 B.C.—Juvenile literature. I. Title. II. Series.
HQ1137.E3S5 2005
305.4'0932—dc22 2004017107

Printed in the United States of America
10 9 8 7 6 5 4 3 2 1

Contents

Foreword

The story of the past as told in traditional historical writings all too often leaves the impression that if men are not the only actors in the narrative, they are assuredly the main characters. With a few notable exceptions, males were the political, military, and economic leaders in virtually every culture throughout recorded time. Since traditional historical scholarship focuses on the public arenas of government, foreign relations, and commerce, the actions and ideas of men—or at least of powerful men—are naturally at the center of conventional accounts of the past.

In the last several decades, however, many historians have abandoned their predecessors' emphasis on "great men" to explore the past "from the bottom up," a phenomenon that has had important consequences for the study of women's history. These social historians, as they are known, focus on the day–to–day experiences of the "silent majority"—those people typically omitted from conventional scholarship because they held relatively little political or economic sway within their societies. In the new social history, members of ethnic and racial minorities, factory workers, peasants, slaves, children, and women are no longer relegated to the background but are placed at the very heart of the narrative.

Around the same time social historians began broadening their research to include women and other previously neglected elements of society, the feminist movement of the late 1960s and 1970s was also bringing unprecedented attention to the female heritage. Feminists hoped that by examining women's past experiences, contemporary women could better understand why and how gender–based expectations had developed in their societies, as well as how they might reshape inherited—and typically restrictive—economic, social, and political roles in the future.

Today, some four decades after the feminist and social history movements gave new impetus to the study of women's history, there is a rich and continually growing body of work on all aspects of women's lives in the past. The Lucent Books Women in History series draws upon this abundant and diverse literature to introduce students to women's experiences within a variety of past cultures and time periods in terms of the distinct roles they filled. In their capacities as workers, activists, and artists, women exerted significant influence on important events whether they conformed to or broke from traditional roles. The Women in History titles depict extraordinary women who managed to attain positions of influence in their male–dominated societies, including such celebrated heroines as the feisty medieval queen Eleanor of Aquitaine, the brilliant propagandist of the American Revolution Mercy Otis Warren, and the courageous African American activist of the Civil War era Harriet Tubman. Included as well are the stories of the ordinary—and often overlooked—women of the past who also helped shape their societies myriad ways—moral, intellectual, and economic—without straying far from customary gender roles: the housewives and mothers, schoolteachers and church volunteers, midwives and nurses, and wartime camp followers.

In this series, readers will discover that many of these unsung women took more significant parts in the great political and social upheavals of their day than has often been recognized. In *Women of the American Revolution,* for example, students will learn how American housewives assumed a crucial role in helping the Patriots win the war against Britain. They accomplished this by planting and harvesting fields, producing and trading goods, and doing whatever else was necessary to maintain the family farm or business in the absence of their soldier husbands despite the heavy burden of housekeeping and child–care duties they already bore. By their self–sacrificing actions, competence, and ingenuity, these anonymous heroines not only kept their families alive, but kept the economy of their struggling young nation going as well during eight long years of war.

Each volume in this series contains generous commentary from the works of respected contemporary scholars, but the Women in History series particularly emphasizes quotations from primary sources such as diaries, letters, and journals whenever possible to allow the women of the past to speak for themselves. These firsthand accounts not only help students to better understand the dimensions of women's daily spheres—the work they did, the organizations they belonged to, the physical hardships they faced—but also how they viewed themselves and their actions in the light of their society's expectations for their sex.

The distinguished American historian Mary Beard once wrote that women have always been a "force in history." It is hoped that the books in this series will help students to better appreciate the vital yet often little–known ways in which women of the past have shaped their societies and cultures.

Introduction: "She Was in Every Respect His Equal"

More than seven thousand years ago, one of the world's greatest civilizations grew up along the banks of the Nile River in a land that would be called Egypt. For historians and the general public alike, ancient Egypt has always been a fascinating place. Historian Brian M. Fagan elaborates on Egypt's appeal: "Ancient Egypt casts a magic spell. . . . All the ingredients of adventure and romance lie along the Nile: golden pharaoh's tombs, high pyramids, and spectacular temples."[1] Ancient Egypt was also the largest literate civilization in the ancient world, causing the Greeks and Romans to call Egypt the birthplace of civilization.

The Rights of Women

Flourishing for more than three thousand years, longer than most other civilizations in world history, ancient Egypt was the only early society that featured equal rights for women. According to Egyptian historians, "This amount of freedom was at variance with that of the Greek woman who required a designated male, called a *kouris*, to represent or stand for her in all legal contracts and proceedings."[2] Indeed, in other areas of the ancient world, women were legally and socially inferior to men in all matters and held only those rights accorded them by male–oriented cultures. Women in Egypt, however, enjoyed a nearly equal status with men, along with unparalleled freedom and responsibility.

In ancient Egypt, women functioned as equals in business, law, medicine, and government. Journalist Rumoko Rashidi describes women's position in Egyptian society: "Women inherited and willed fortunes . . . introduced legislation at the courts of law and commanded the respect of king and commoner alike."[3]

Ancient Egyptian women could own property, a right not granted in other societies until hundreds, if not thousands, of years later. They were also equally accountable under the law and could serve as witnesses, plaintiffs, defendants, or attorneys in court with the same rights

Queen Nefertiti, Pharaoh Akhenaton, and their daughters pray to the sun god in this carving. The women of ancient Egypt typically enjoyed equal rights with men.

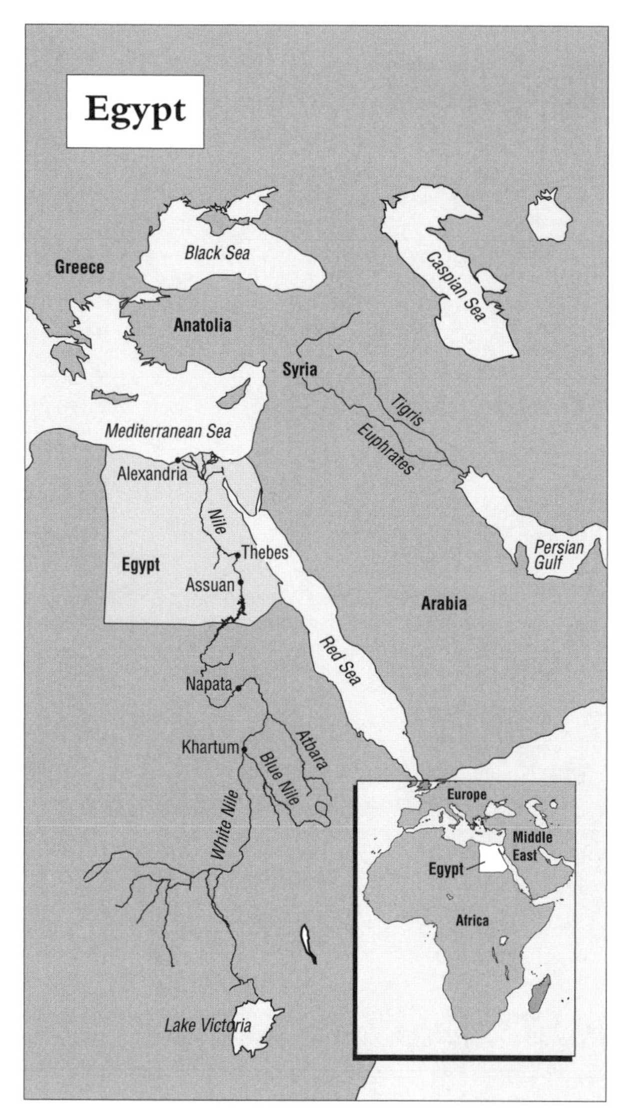

as Egyptian men. Ancient Egyptian women also had the right to hold important positions within the government and business world, and they could be financially independent of their husbands.

These rights and responsibilities of women were divided along class lines rather than gender lines. Egyptian society was extremely class conscious. The king, or pharaoh, held the top position in Egyptian society, with his family and members of the royalty coming next. Following the royalty in importance were members of the upper class, or nobility, most of whom held positions in government, business, and religion. The peasant class, the most populous segment of society, came next, followed by slaves, who occupied the lowest rank in Egyptian society. In nearly all cases, a woman's social position was defined by that of her class. Rights and privileges were not uniform from one class to another, but within the given classes equal rights were accorded to both men and women.

Rights Within the Family

In the domestic sphere, men and women enjoyed equal responsibilities and rights within a marriage, and both were expected to fulfill certain obligations. Once married, for instance, a man was expected to provide for his wife, and the woman was responsible for the house and children. Historian James Henry Breasted explains the way marriages in ancient Egypt worked: "A man possessed but one legal wife, who was the mother of his heirs. She was in every respect his equal, was always treated with the greatest consideration."[4]

Women were allowed to divorce their husbands in ancient Egypt, a right usually not accorded to women in other ancient societies. All that divorce required was for the wife to leave her husband and move back into her parents' home. Divorce was handled quietly as a private matter between the couple, leaving the state and the courts no role in the proceedings. Divorce was quite common in ancient Egypt and had no stigma attached to it. Almost any excuse could be used to end a marriage. The most common was the inability of the couple to conceive a child. Although either spouse might be the cause for infertility, responsibility for the failure to conceive was generally placed on the woman. Husbands, as a result, were allowed to leave their wives in order to find another woman who could provide them with children. In addition, spouses could divorce if they believed they were being neglected or physically abused by the other.

Divorced Egyptian women had the right to receive alimony in the form of full financial support until they remarried. As a rule, Egyptian wives took custody of the children and also retained all of their own personal property. Remarriage was common in ancient Egypt since living alone was both difficult and unacceptable according to strictly defined social customs.

Whether married or divorced, ancient Egyptian women were able to make positive contributions to Egyptian society because of their equality, rights, and responsibilities. As a result, women played many important roles in the early years of Egyptian history. They held important positions within the government, influenced male leaders, and became powerful figures. Others worked behind the scenes in the villages and in various professions, helping Egyptian civilization attain its greatness. A few even became pharaoh and successfully ruled Egypt during times of both war and peace.

Throughout its three–thousand–year history, ancient Egypt flourished and thrived as one of the most enlightened and civilized societies anywhere in the world. Nowhere else did women play such a significant and equal role in society. Their exalted position during this period would diminish severely after the death of Cleopatra VII in 30 B.C. It would be thousands of years before women would come close to holding the same status and freedom that they possessed during the ancient Egyptian empire.

Chapter 1: The Peasant Woman

Nearly 80 percent of the estimated 5 million people who lived in ancient Egypt were peasants. It has been difficult for archaeologists and historians to learn about the lives of ancient Egyptian peasants. The peasants left no elaborate graves to preserve their history; as a result, archaeologists have had to rely on various tomb paintings and other art forms to learn about their lives. Funerary monuments such as tombs and statues that depict large households typically show peasant women carrying out household tasks such as grinding grain, baking bread, and brewing beer. Remains of pottery have also given historians a glimpse of ancient life. A National Public Radio broadcaster explains why this kind of art is so important in understanding Egyptian life: "Basically what you're seeing are the stories of the people who built the tombs, who built the temples: . . . [These stories bring] ancient Egypt to life."[5]

While their husbands worked in the vast agricultural fields or on building projects for the pharaoh, peasant women stayed home and were responsible for maintaining the house and rearing the children. They lived a hard and short life, averaging around thirty years. Most women died in the same villages and farms where they were born, never venturing more than a few miles from their home. Their days were long ones, often beginning well before dawn and continuing well into the night. The number of tasks they performed was nearly endless and included everything from baking bread to making clothing, doing laundry to caring for the livestock, and helping with the harvest to nursing sick family members. These roles and responsibilities remained virtually unchanged during the three thousand years that compose ancient Egyptian history.

Preparing for the Day's Work

A peasant woman's day began before dawn, when she arose from her mattress or sleeping mat. Because of the extremely hot climate of Egypt and the stifling conditions inside houses, she and her family generally slept on the roof of their home, where they could take advantage of the nighttime breeze. Once up, the woman generally began her day by preparing the morning meal, usually consisting of some kind of cereal or grain. Her family members ate separately whenever they got up; breakfast usually was not a time when the family gathered together.

Following breakfast, the peasant woman bathed and dressed in preparation for her long day. Her first activity was to go to a nearby stream, where she used a mix of ash and animal fat, an inexpensive version of soap, to clean her body. She might also use a deodorant made of turpentine and incense. Cleanliness was important to all Egyptians, and all peasants bathed daily. After bathing, a peasant woman dressed in a simple white dress made of coarse linen and began her work.

Cooking and Baking Bread

A peasant woman spent a large portion of each day cooking for her family. Her most time–consuming task was making and baking bread from emmer wheat and barley, the two major crops of Egypt. Bread was the most important item in the Egyptian diet and provided the main source of protein for the ancient Egyptians. Historians have discovered numerous recipes for making bread and believe more than fifty different types of bread were consumed in Egypt.

Making bread was a long process, sometimes taking several hours. It had to be done on a daily basis since the loaves quickly became dry and stale in the hot Egyptian climate. With no way to keep most food fresh in ancient Egypt, a woman had to prepare the majority of each meal from scratch. To turn grain into usable flour, she had to pound and then grind the wheat. The grain was pounded

An Egyptian wall painting depicts peasant women fishing and hunting game. The peasant women of ancient Egypt led short and very difficult lives.

This wooden figurine shows a peasant woman using a stone to grind wheat for bread. Egyptian women spent many tedious hours each day making loaves of bread from scratch.

with a smooth rock, and a simple stone or clay handmill was used to grind or crush the grain.

The woman usually added a little sand to the grain to help in the grinding process. Sand added weight and consistency to the grain, thus making it easier to grind. This combination, however, left a gritty residue that caused multiple dental problems for the Egyptians. Historians, through an examination of the mouths of mummies, have confirmed that the sand often wore ancient Egyptian teeth thin. After the grinding process, the peasant woman put the grain through a sieve that further refined it until it produced a powder that had the consistency of flour. With no sugar available in ancient Egypt, women usually flavored and sweetened the bread by adding honey, fruit, nuts, or palm oil.

Women kneaded the bread into a variety of shapes and then baked it in a cylindrical clay oven that was usually located either on the home's roof or in an outside courtyard. The oven was placed in these locations to keep smoke from entering the house. The poorest women, unable to afford a clay oven, instead baked their bread in special clay containers over an open fire. All women used straw and animal dung to light the fires and ovens. In addition to bread, women also made a wide variety of pastries and cakes.

Preparing Food

The typical Egyptian peasant woman also prepared many other kinds of food to serve during the main meal, usually held in the evening when the entire family could gather together. Women grew a variety of vegetables in small gardens near their homes and used these in many recipes. The vegetables included such items as leeks, onions, garlic, cucumbers, lettuce, cabbage, and radishes as well as a variety of beans, which were served raw, boiled, or steamed. Onions and garlic were a major part of the ancient Egyptian diet and were used in many vegetable dishes. Cabbage, considered a delicacy,

Egyptian Agriculture

Peasants formed the backbone of Egypt's vast agricultural industry. The majority of ancient Egyptian peasants worked as farmers on large estates owned by either the state or wealthy noblemen. The peasants who worked the land received little reward for their work, although most produced enough to feed themselves and their families.

It was the yearly flood that gave Egypt its rich farm land by leaving behind silt that was extremely fertile. By October or November, the Nile deposited a thick layer of black silt that covered the ground. Wooden plows were used to break up the rich, moist soil before it was sown with seeds. The primary crops were barley and wheat, although corn was also produced in quantity. Flax was also grown and provided the material for Egyptian clothing. Dates, grapes, and other fruits and vegetables were also harvested during the growing year.

Once the seeds were planted, the most important task during the hot, dry summer was to keep the land irrigated. Canals were dug from the Nile River, and a device called a *shaduf* was used to get water to the fields. The *shaduf* consisted of a beam with a weight on one end and a bucket on the other. A man or woman dipped the bucket into the river, let the weight pull it up, and poured water into the irrigating canals. This device is still used in Egypt today.

was also popular and could be boiled and eaten before the rest of the meal. Egyptian women also used a number of spices, such as cumin, anise, dill, thyme, sage, and marjoram, to add flavor to the vegetables.

Peasant women served a variety of fruits for the evening meal, the most common being grapes, figs, melons, dates, and pomegranates. They did not have access to such produce as peaches, pears, and cherries, for these fruits had to be imported, making them very expensive and available only to wealthy families. A woman could easily spend several hours a day picking the fruits that were available in her area off nearby trees and vines. She either used them in recipes for her own family or took them to the market, where she traded them for other items.

Instead of eating red meat, an item that was expensive and affordable only by the very rich, the peasant class usually ate fish, which the woman served boiled, fried, roasted, or dried. Peasant women also cooked wild birds like ducks and geese, which their husbands caught and killed. Quails, ducks, and smaller birds were salted and eaten raw, whereas other kinds of birds were eaten either roasted or boiled. Any fish or bird that was not immediately eaten was prepared for storage by salting and drying it in the sun. The woman then packed the food in ashes and placed it under her house for preservation and later consumption. The same process was followed for preserving vegetables; these were generally stored in pots, bags, and baskets. Many of these containers had handles so they could be suspended from the ceiling in order to prevent rodents and insects from getting in the food.

Cooking and Meals

Cooking was hard and tiring work for the peasant women of ancient Egypt. They had only a few simple tools, including clay pots, bone spoons, and stone knives to help them in the preparation of food. Other items, such as pans, storage jars, ladles, and straw whisks, might also be found in a peasant woman's kitchen. To mix or slice most food, a woman would place the dishes on the floor and then crouch or sit on the ground beside them.

When she needed to use water, the peasant woman had to carry it from the Nile River or its tributaries. Some women were fortunate to have streams or canals close to their homes, but others had to travel a mile or more several times a day. She usually carried the water in homemade baskets and clay containers. Goat skins were also used for transporting water.

Food was generally eaten with the fingers, although a few families possessed clay knives, spoons, forks, and plates. These items had to be obtained at the market since peasant women could not afford to build pottery kilns in their homes and make their own utensils. More commonly, however, food was placed in a large bowl on the floor and each person in the family used a piece of bread to scoop up his or her meal. Meat and fish were nibbled directly off the bones. Any dishes that were used were then washed in the river, a task that peasant women performed before retiring for the night.

Making Beer

In addition to cooking and preparing food for family consumption, Egyptian women also made the most common drink consumed in Egypt—beer. Egyptian myth taught the people that Osiris, one of the most important Egyptian gods, taught humans how to brew beer. In keeping with this idea, the Egyptians often used beer in religious ceremonies and as the main mealtime beverage. Records indicate that nearly twenty different kinds of beer were made in Egypt. The Egyptians were so proficient at making this beverage that, as historians Bob Brier and Hoyt Hobbs state, "[beer,] produced from the earliest days in Egypt, is generally considered to be an Egyptian invention."[6]

It was the peasant woman's responsibility to make the beer her family consumed. When barley bread was about half-baked, the woman took it from her oven and mixed it with water in large earthenware jugs and added honey for a sweet flavor. She placed these jugs in the sun until the mixture had time to ferment, or change into a form of alcohol. During this process, the liquid became fizzy and very thick, looking a bit like muddy soup. Once the mixture had fermented over a period of two to three days, women filtered the resulting product with sieves and stored it in jars or containers.

Egyptian beer was widely consumed by all classes of people. It was also, by far, the safest beverage to consume. Ancient Egypt's river water was rife with bacteria, often making it dangerous to drink. Scientists today acknowledge that the alcohol content of Egyptian beer killed any bacteria, thus rendering it safer to drink than plain water. Egyptian beer tasted like cider or fizzy soda and was not nearly as alcoholic as drinks are today; as a result, it did not produce any ill effects.

Weaving and Spinning

A peasant woman was also responsible for spinning thread and weaving it into clothes for herself and her family. She also made sleeping rugs, simple blankets, and towels. In these tasks, she might work side by side with other women by using her home's courtyard as a kind of workshop area where, together, the women could make clothing, sandals, and other items. The women usually hung thick cloth awnings on poles to protect themselves and the cloth from the hot sun while they worked.

An ancient wooden model depicts a scene in a weaver's workshop, in which women spin flax and weave the thread into clothes and textiles.

The everyday clothing worn by peasants was usually made of unbleached linen. This material came from flax, a plant that was cultivated in Egypt because of its strong and flexible fibers. Peasant women pulled the flax from the ground and then soaked the stems for several days to separate the fibers. Afterward, they pounded the material with stones or simple bone tools until the fiber was soft enough to be straightened out in thread form. They used a simple loom for weaving. The loom was made of two beams that were held in place by four pegs driven into the ground.

Women also made clothing from sheep wool, goat skins, and cow leather. Women performed all of the tasks associated with the production of clothing from these items, from shearing the sheep to sewing the pieces together with small bone needles and thread. Using sharpened stone knives or crude razors made of bone, peasant women sheared the family's sheep once or twice a year. Once the wool was collected, it was spun to produce thread that could be used to make warm clothing. Woolen capes and simple coats were made for peasants to wear during the cooler night hours in Egypt.

Women at Work

When not working on their farms, thousands of peasant women joined their husbands and worked for the government building temples, pyramids, and other structures. Some made the sun–dried bricks used in the building process, and others carried small loads of other construction materials. Still others were responsible for preparing food and drink for the entire crew.

While working on these projects, women lived with their families in small villages built for the workers. These villages featured marketplaces where families could obtain simple foodstuffs and other products. Archaeologists have, in recent years, uncovered the remains of many of these villages. At El–Amarna, for example, the workers' houses were small, barracklike buildings. In his article "Valley of the Kings," *National Geographic* journalist Kent R. Weeks reports on the excavations at another village: "More than three thousand years ago, Deir el–Medina was home to a hundred sculptors, woodworkers, quarrymen, painters, and plasterers. They lived with their wives and children in nearly seventy single–story houses strung along a lane hardly wide enough for two donkeys to pass."

While men were usually responsible for the slaughter of livestock, peasant women took charge of tanning cow and goat skins and using them to make clothing and other items. Women stretched the skins between simple pegs hammered into the ground, scraped any flesh off the skins, and allowed them to dry in the sun. The skin, or leather, was then cut with flint knives and made into various items. Women also used the skins to make carrying containers that resembled sacks and used them for transporting different wares to the marketplace. They were also useful for carrying water from place to place.

Making Baskets

In addition to cooperative sewing ventures, women also gathered together to make baskets, which were widely used in peasant homes. Historian Rosalie David describes why baskets were so important: "Baskets were indispensable for storing domestic items and for carrying agricultural and industrial materials."[7] The baskets were also popular market items that could be traded for other goods.

To make baskets, peasant women cut down the abundant plants that grew along the riverbank. Tall, grasslike plants known as rushes were the primary materials used, although scientists have identified more than one hundred different kinds of plants that grew in ancient Egypt that were used at one time or another in the weaving process.

Coiling was the primary method women used for making baskets and other products. A woman would gather hundreds of reed fibers and then wind them into a flat coil in order to make the base of the basket. She then built it up by wrapping the fibers spirally and fixing each row to the previous one by stitching them together with other plant fibers. Egyptian historians explain this process: "In coiling, cordage is formed of braided or twisted strands of plant fiber, coiled into a . . . spiral, and sewn together, resulting . . . in a mat or basket."[8]

In making a mat, for instance, the coils were placed on a flat surface and then wound around until the product was complete. A basket was made differently; the coils were formed and wound one upon each other until the desired height was reached. These methods are still used today by basketmakers around the world.

Helping with the Harvest

The baskets made by peasant women were also used during the harvest, which was a time of great activity for the peasants of ancient Egypt. The farmer's year was generally split into three seasons: the inundation, or *akhet*, was the period during which the Nile flooded the valleys; this occurred during the months from July to November. The second season was

The harvest was a busy time for all Egyptian peasants. In this wall painting, peasant women bundle into sheaves the grain harvested by the men.

the growing season, or *peret*, usually from November to March. During this time, women helped their husbands plant the fields by scattering seeds from handmade wicker baskets that were slung over their shoulders for easy access. Archaeologists have discovered numerous tomb paintings that depict peasant women helping with the harvest by picking wheat and flax and by carrying baskets of crops from the field to the storehouse.

The harvest, or *shomu*, occurred between March and July and was, by far, the busiest time of the year. Every able–bodied villager was needed during the harvest. Men used sickles to cut stalks of wheat and corn. Women and children bundled the cut materials into sheaves

A statuette depicts a loving Egyptian family. Women served as the primary caregivers for families in ancient Egypt.

and packed them into baskets, and other women gleaned. Gleaning consisted of going over the ground and picking up anything the other workers had missed, including ears of corn or even single grains—nothing was wasted. The corn or wheat was then broken down or threshed, a process that turned it into grain. The grain was then taken to the granary, where it was stored. Women were responsible for storing the grain and giving it out in small amounts to each family so that the crop lasted all year long.

Caring for Children and Family

In addition to being responsible for a variety of daily tasks, peasant women were the primary caregivers for their children and other family members. Most peasant families were large and included numerous children. With her husband gone most of the day, working in the fields or on building projects, the responsibility for teaching and disciplining the children fell to the mother. Working mothers often carried their children with them while going to the market or while working in the fields. Grandparents, who usually lived with the family, also played a role in the upbringing of children, watching and caring for them while parents were occupied elsewhere. Despite some help received with the children, it ultimately remained the peasant mother's responsibility to care for and rear her children.

The peasant mother educated her children. She taught her young children, especially her daughters, what their roles in society would be. In order to reinforce these roles, children were separated by gender by around the age of four to six years. A peasant girl's life in ancient Egypt was much different than a boy's. Daughters were taught that their lives would center around their homes and families. Egyptian historians describe some of the things young girls were taught: "At age four, girls would begin to learn from their mothers how to maintain the house. They would learn how to sew, make foods, and keep house."[9] Egyptian boys, on the other hand, were sent to work in the fields with their fathers, where their roles in life were reinforced by working and spending time with the men.

A peasant woman also took physical care of her children. When they were sick, she nursed them back to health by mixing herbal medicines, saying prayers, and reciting various spells. Most women were experts at treating a variety of ills with herbal concoctions they had been taught to make by their mothers and grandmothers. A peasant woman was also able to set broken bones, stitch up various cuts, and provide healing salves to rub on her children's abrasions and burns.

In addition to rearing children and providing for their medical treatment, a peasant woman also made many of the toys with which her children played. The most common items she made were dolls. These were made of reeds or small pieces of wood and then adorned in dresses made from cloth that was left over from the production of family clothes. The dolls were then stuffed with plant fibers to add bulk and shape.

Cleaning and Washing

In addition to caring for her children's well–being, a good portion of a peasant woman's day was spent keeping her house clean and washing the family's clothing. These chores were made difficult by the kinds of homes in which the Egyptians lived. Windblown sand and the prevalence of numerous insects and other pests further complicated the maintenance of clean homes.

Most peasants lived in one– or two–story houses that were cramped and crowded and usually located in a maze of winding, dusty streets in small villages along the Nile. These homes were made of mud brick and featured small, dark rooms with narrow windows and low ceilings. These homes were usually built close together and fell apart quite easily because of the damaging floodwaters of the Nile and the harsh sun. Mud often flaked off the exterior building, bricks eroded, and

Women balance baskets of clothing on their heads as they walk to the Nile. Washing clothes in the river was dangerous, as hungry crocodiles were often found along its shores.

inside walls cracked and crumbled, making it necessary to repair and rebuild on a near–constant basis. The very poor could not even afford these kinds of homes; they often lived in one–room reed huts.

Sand was a constant nuisance, blowing in off the nearby desert, covering everything, and getting into the smallest of places. It was virtually impossible to keep the fine grains out of the home. As a result, peasant women usually had to sweep the floors two or three times a day. They used reed brushes that had no handles, requiring them to bend low when sweeping.

Women also had to constantly keep the house free of flies, mice, and scorpions that might pose a danger to their families. To prevent being stung by deadly scorpions, which liked to hide in small, dark places, women shook out items they were cleaning rather than inserting their hands into them. There was little the woman could do, however, to prevent black flies from invading her home: these seemed to be everywhere. To keep the insects out of foodstuffs, everything was stored in baskets or cloth and leather containers.

Another part of a peasant woman's day was spent washing clothes. Although the wealthy used professional men who ran laundries on the banks of the Nile, the poor washed their own clothes. For washing, peasant women pounded the wet clothes against rocks while using a soapy mix made from ashes, called lye. This method was extremely hard on the hands and resulted in frequent abrasions, burns, and dry skin. While washing clothes women also constantly had to be on the lookout for crocodiles, which lived in the rivers and marshes of Egypt. Once she had washed the clothes, the peasant woman laid them out on rocks to whiten and dry them in the sun.

Caring for Livestock

In addition to her other household duties, the Egyptian peasant woman was also kept busy each day caring for the sheep, goats, and pets the family owned. Most peasant families kept a small number of animals to help with certain tasks as well as to provide milk, meat, and wool for food and clothing. Oxen, for instance, were used in the harvesting process, and donkeys often provided transportation or assistance in pulling things.

These animals were highly prized and were treated as indispensable members of the family. Peasant women were very knowledgeable about how to care for them and how to best meet their needs. Historians describe some of the specialized knowledge that women possessed: "Those who kept animals knew them well—their mating habits, their diet and growth, their ailments, and all their characteristics."[10]

Pets were kept not so much for the companionship they provided as for their usefulness to the family. Cats, for instance, were quite valuable in ancient Egypt because of their ability to catch and kill rodents. Dogs were trained to help in the hunting of wild birds and also to pull small loads of grain, vegetables, or other items. Peasant women took charge of keeping the animals clean and fed. They often served as veterinarians by keeping their pets healthy. They knew how to set animal bones, perform simple surgeries such as stitching a small wound, and treat a variety of other ills.

Going to the Marketplace

In addition to all her other responsibilities, peasant women were required to visit the marketplace at least once a week. This trip could take anywhere from a few hours to an entire day. The peasant woman walked to the market, a journey of at least several miles, carrying her wares in a basket placed on her head. The items she took to market usually included eggs, baskets, or homemade mats that she could sell or trade.

A woman had to do a lot of bargaining at the marketplace to obtain the things she needed for her family. Since peasants rarely used money, anything the woman wanted to purchase had to be traded for. She might, for instance, trade a dozen eggs for a small clay pot or a homemade basket for different fruits and vegetables that were imported from another region of Egypt. Other items she might acquire included fresh meat, kitchen implements, and simple herbal medicines.

The peasant woman played a number of important roles in Egyptian society. She was responsible for taking care of her family, feeding them, nurturing them, and providing them with clothing and medical care. In the community, she helped with the harvest and enjoyed the fellowship of other women as they made a variety of goods for family use and for selling in the market. In fulfilling all of these roles, the peasant woman was indispensable to the well–being of her family, her community, and Egyptian society.

Chapter 2: A Life of Luxury and Leisure

Wealthy women of the noble class enjoyed a life of luxury and leisure characterized by the finest clothing, jewelry, and accommodations. They played an active role in the domestic sphere, where they were responsible for rearing children, running vast households, and overseeing servants. With their husbands frequently away from home running businesses and other ventures, wealthy women often ran large estates on their own for months at a time. Because of these responsibilities and others, women of wealth were held in high regard and were respected throughout the Egyptian empire. Historian David Silverman elaborates: "Although Ancient Egyptian society was male–dominated, the frequency with which elite women were depicted alongside their husbands and sons shows that they were recognized as playing an important role within society."[11]

Mistress of the House

As mistress of the house, wealthy women were responsible for ensuring the proper maintenance and elegance of their homes. They lived amid the finest furnishings, and compared to the poorer people of Egypt, they lived a luxurious and pampered life. Many of their homes were like miniature estates, with each spouse having his or her own separate living quarters. The mistress usually had her own receiving room for meeting and entertaining her friends and the wives of other important rich men.

Every rich woman surrounded herself with the most beautiful furnishings possible. To do otherwise would be perceived as unacceptable by class standards; thus, women often competed with one another to possess the finest furniture and other decorations. Homes were often equipped with pillars, high ceilings, tiled floors, and luxurious carpets so that a visitor's first impression was a good one. All bedrooms were furnished with wooden beds covered with woven mats. Impressive stone, wooden or bamboo chests stored linens, clothing, jewelry, and makeup.

Egyptian women loved beautiful objects and usually filled their homes with a variety of rich and ornate decorations. One of the most popular was a dazzling blue pottery called faience. In addition, wealthy women collected jars made of a white stone called alabaster and adorned their walls with colorful paintings and other works of art.

Many wealthy women possessed their own bathrooms, allowing them the luxury of relieving themselves in the privacy of their own homes. These rooms featured simple "indoor plumbing," complete with a toilet with stone or wooden seats and an opening placed above a tray of sand. To further enhance her comfort, a small stool with a similar pan of sand was placed at her bedside for nighttime use. The sand was emptied and changed by the servants each morning. These facilities were quite different from those used by peasants. Peasant women used primitive outdoor buildings when available; otherwise, they relieved themselves anywhere there was a little privacy.

Overseeing Servants

Rarely did wealthy women actually clean and maintain their luxurious homes. Instead, they relied exclusively on a large retinue of servants or slaves to perform all the necessary household tasks. It was a rich woman's responsibility to oversee the servants. She hired them, evaluated their performance, and took care of all other issues relating to their upkeep and effectiveness. By taking care of all these tasks, a woman ensured that her household ran efficiently. Without servants, the lives of the wealthy would have been very different and much less luxurious. "So dependent were the upper classes on their household help," write the editors of Time–Life Books, "that they equipped their burial chambers with statuettes of attendants to wait on them in the afterlife."[12]

The female servants and slaves who reported to the mistress of the house came primarily from peasant families who did not have enough land or other work to support themselves. A wealthy woman often hired the wives of various tenant farmers who already worked and lived on her land. While female servants were free to come and go depending on their needs, slaves belonged to the mistress and could be bought and sold like property. For the most part, however, slaves were extremely valued and, therefore, well treated. Unlike slaves in other parts of the ancient world, Egyptian slaves could own property, marry, and even buy their own freedom. A few more–fortunate slaves were adopted by their owners, and a privileged few eventually became the heirs to large estates.

Female servants were indispensable to their mistresses and performed a wide variety of tasks for them. In addition to

Wealthy Women as Property Owners

Many wealthy women owned property independently of their husbands. In addition, upon the deaths of their husbands, many women inherited large tracts of land and estates. Propertied women ran these estates and holdings on their own. A scroll discovered in Egypt, dating to 1156 B.C., shows, in fact, that 10 percent of all Egyptian land and property belonged to women.

Being able to own or rent property of their own meant that Egyptian women were not totally economically dependent on their husbands. This financial independence allowed many women to prosper during their lifetimes and after the death of their spouses. With money of their own, Egyptian women were able to make bargains, figure accounts, lend money, and buy or sell land. When writing a will for her children, an Egyptian woman could also leave part of her property to her daughters.

The labor of slaves like those depicted in this wooden carving created a life of luxury and ease for the wealthy women of ancient Egypt.

their cleaning duties, servants helped their mistresses bathe, dress, apply makeup, and put on jewelry. They were responsible for getting rid of household waste and garbage, which was dumped in the street or in a nearby canal. Many wealthy women also employed servants to breast-feed their children.

The wealthy woman was also responsible for a staff of yardmen who tended her family's vast gardens. Many of these gardens featured man-made pools that were filled with brightly colored and exotic fish. Women purchased the fish and other pool items at nearby markets or imported them from foreign lands. Flowers, floating plants, orchids, and other forms of ornamentation were used to decorate the gardens and exteriors of the homes. The wealthy woman was also responsible for overseeing the maintenance of any small summerhouses on the estate. These houses were set aside for the use of guests and were also used by the family for relaxation and shelter during the heat of the day.

Each wealthy woman provided ample living space for her female servants, usually in a building somewhere on the estate. Many rich families built special blocks of servant's quarters away from the main house. Women also made sure that their servants were provided with food and clothing during the length of their employment. In addition to providing room and board, wealthy women paid their female servants, usually with linen, food, kitchen tools, or furniture that could be shared with the servant's family.

Entertaining Others

In addition to maintaining an elegant home and overseeing the household help,

A female servant fastens a brooch around her mistress's neck. Servants were responsible for a wide variety of domestic tasks.

wealthy Egyptian women were responsible for hosting banquets and dinners for their important friends. Entertainment played a large role in the life of the rich Egyptian, and there was much competition between wealthy families to put on the largest and most luxurious party in the community. A wealthy man relied on his wife to plan these events in order to make his banquet a worthy and impressive affair. Rich women made every effort to see that the rooms used for these parties were beautifully decorated with furniture, expensive artwork, and fresh flowers.

In order to impress her banquet guests, wealthy Egyptian women also paid careful attention to their appearance. They were often dressed in flowing linen gowns that reached the floor. Once properly dressed, the mistress of the house greeted each guest individually and welcomed them to the festivities, often draping the guest in colorful wreaths of flowers. Many hostesses carried lotus flowers themselves and wore elaborate and perfumed wigs to add fragrance and elegance to the occasion.

A wealthy woman was expected to plan the banquet menu and then ensure that her staff of servants prepared the food and presented it in an attractive manner. Most of the dinners and banquets were elaborate productions in which everyone either sat on the floor or at individual round tables. After everyone was properly seated, servants carried in breads of many shapes and varieties, whole roasted chickens and turkeys, joints of meat, several kinds of vegetables, and assorted fruits for the individual guests. A variety of different wines was also served with the meal, along with elegant desserts. During the meal, women were expected to remain quiet or talk softly among themselves. Depending on the type of banquet being planned and whether it was a business dinner or a social one, women might either join the entire group or sit separately from the men. A wealthy woman was expected to set an example for her female guests and behave in a subdued and proper manner, leaving the men to discuss whatever business drew them together.

Following the meal, the mistress of the house made sure that her guests were shown to their overnight accommodations. Many banquets lasted well into the night, so guests were usually provided with rooms in which to rest. By arranging a successful dinner party, a wealthy woman enhanced her husband's position in the community.

The Importance of Fashion and Appearance

Just as they worked to present the best possible appearance at banquets and dinners, wealthy Egyptian women also placed great importance on daily appearance and fashion. They had a highly developed sense of personal beauty and took great care in every aspect of their appearance. Historian Joann Fletcher elaborates on the need for presenting a good appearance: "Appearances were of paramount importance and . . . developed from a sense of practicality combined with a love of beauty."[13] Good hygiene and grooming habits played an important part of the lives of the elite and reflected people of good breeding. The way a woman dressed and looked, in fact, indicated her status, role in society, and political significance.

The importance of appearance is reflected in the imagery used in ancient Egyptian art. For women, the ideal was youthful beauty. As a result, pregnant, elderly, and obese women were rarely depicted. The typical image, instead, was of a full–figured young woman dressed in a flowing white gown with her hair immaculately prepared and decorated with flower blossoms. Tomb paintings depict women wearing the latest fashions in wigs, clothing, and makeup. In every aspect of her appearance, an Egyptian woman radiated beauty, poise, and elegance. Many historians agree that Egyptian women were recognized throughout the ancient world for their beauty.

An elegantly dressed Queen Nefertari appears with the goddess Isis in this wall painting.

Women and Their Clothing

To enhance their appearance, rich women wore nothing but the finest and most expensive white linen clothing. Their dresses were simple but elegant and were so well made that many of them were nearly transparent, a sign of the very best linen and craftsmanship. Only wealthy women could afford the type of expensive cloth that produced this effect. Historian James Henry Breasted describes a typical dress worn by a noblewoman: "They were clothed in a thin, close–fitting, sleeveless, white linen garment hanging from the breast to the ankles, and supported by two bands passing over the shoulders. . . . A long wig, a collar and necklace, and a pair of bracelets completed the lady's costume."[14]

Wealthy women hired dressmakers to make and design all of their clothing. Female dressmakers obtained the necessary lengths of linen and then showed the rich woman how to wear it most attractively. The fabric usually consisted of nothing but a rectangle, four times as long as it was wide and often exceeding seventy–five feet in length. Garments were draped around the wearer instead of sewn into a form–fitting mold. Several different methods of draping produced a variety of looks. Many women wore their dresses in a manner similar to Indian saris, with one corner tucked into the waist. Others liked their dresses to have pleats; these were formed by pressing a damp cloth into the material and then leaving it to dry folded on a wooden board. The cloth was then wrapped around the back, tossed over one shoulder, and then the other. For added variety, many women preferred to have their linen clothing dyed, using saffron to create a yellow color, iron to make red, and indigo for blue.

In addition to their flowing dresses, many wealthy women wore wool capes and stoles on cool Egyptian nights. These items were made by dressmakers or servants in accordance with the desires of the mistress of the house. The wealthy also often wore sandals made from leather and stitched together with papyrus reed; their poorer counterparts, in contrast, usually went barefoot. Each woman tried to outdo her neighbors and acquaintances in what she wore and how she looked. By putting on the best possible appearance, women enhanced their position in society as well as the status of their husbands.

Face and Eye Care

From the time she got up in the morning, a wealthy Egyptian woman focused on making herself as appealing and beautiful as possible. The affluent washed daily, starting the day with a shower of cool water poured from a servant's pitcher and enriched with cleansing ingredients. The most common of these ingredients was natron, a salty mineral found in lake beds. Following her bath, a woman was thoroughly dried off by a servant, who then applied a generous amount of oil and cream, generally lotus–scented, to keep the lady's skin smooth and soft.

These oils and creams were very important as a protection against the hot sun and dry, sandy winds of Egypt. The use of such products was not considered a luxury but rather a necessity of daily life and were thus used by all classes of ancient Egyptian women. The oils, containing a base of cat, hippopotamus, or crocodile fat, helped keep the skin soft and prevented a woman's skin from becoming dry and cracked. Henna, a

Wealthy women like Queen Nefertari wore dark eye makeup to enhance their beauty and to protect their eyes from the sun and windblown sand.

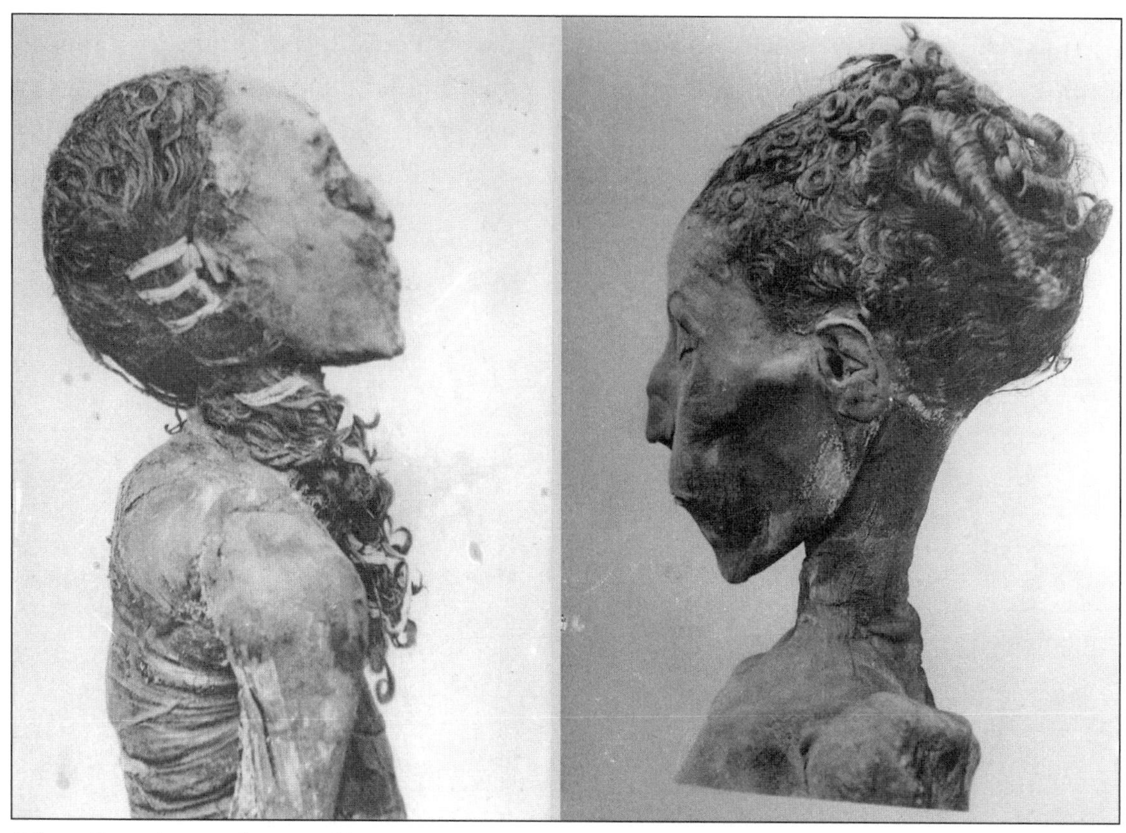

These four–thousand–year–old mummies wearing perfectly preserved wigs made from natural hair were unearthed in Luxor.

reddish–orange dye, was used to redden the palms of the hands and the soles of the feet, helping to protect these areas from the sun and sand.

Although all Egyptian women wore eye makeup, wealthy women made use of the finest materials and chemicals while peasant women used more economical products. The makeup was worn not only for the sake of appearance but also as protection from the desert's beating sun, blowing sand, and swarming flies, all of which could cause eye infections and blindness. To protect their eyes, Egyptian women used a black lead ore called galena, which was ground into powder in a mortar dish. This was then mixed with fat or cream and was stored in a stone pot. The resulting product was called kohl. The mixture, which was expensive and not available to the poor, was applied with a cosmetic spoon. Even more popular than the black eye makeup was green eye paint made from malachite, a copper ore; the green color symbolized fertility. Powdered limestone, mixed with vegetable oil, was used to remove makeup each evening.

Wigs and Hair Care

Most Egyptian men and women shaved their heads bald and replaced their natural hair with wigs. There were many reasons for this practice, as explained by Egyptian historians: "Head shaving had a number of benefits. First, removing their hair made it much more comfortable in the hot Egyptian climate. Second, it was easy to maintain a high degree of cleanliness, avoiding the danger of lice infestation. In addition, people wore wigs when their natural hair was gone due to old age."[15]

The wigs worn by wealthy women were made of human hair and were kept in place with beeswax. Even servant girls and peasants wore wigs, usually made of vegetable fibers, although theirs were not nearly as elaborate as those of the wealthy. Both short and long wigs were

Ancient Egyptian Beauty Tips

To enhance their beauty, ancient Egyptian women developed a large number of beauty aids and cosmetics. Most wealthy women, for instance, wore some kind of deodorant. To prevent body odor, a woman often mixed together an ostrich egg, a tortoise shell, and a gall nut from a tamarisk plant to rub on the body. Others used a deodorant made from ground carob (a chocolate–like tree pod), and an antiwrinkle cream was made from a mixture of frankincense, oil, grass, and fermented fruit juices.

To keep their breath sweet, women mixed together dry frankincense, pine seeds, honey, cashew nut resin, fragrant reed, cinnamon rind, and melon. This mixture was finely ground, mixed into a solid mass, and put on the fire to simmer. After heating, the mixture was made into pellets and sucked, similar to today's breath mints.

Modern scientists have recently discovered that the chemical technology of the ancient Egyptians was far more advanced and sophisticated than previously thought. Some of the products made by the early Egyptians were, scientists conclude, quite effective in their purpose. "The knowledge of the Egyptian physicians to chemistry was so vast," writes medical historian Sameh M. Arab, in his online article "Medicine in Ancient Egypt," "that some would attribute the origin of the word chemistry to Kemet, the ancient name of Egypt."

available in ancient Egypt. Short wigs were made of small curls arranged in overlapping horizontal lines. The forehead was partially visible, but the ears and the back of the neck were fully covered. Long–haired wigs, on the other hand, hung down heavily from the top of the head to below the shoulders. Wealthy women often kept wigs of both lengths for use on different occasions.

Wealthy women preferred their wigs to be intricately designed and enhanced with fragrant oils, pieces of wood chips, cinnamon, or flower petals. Some rich women decorated their wigs with threaded gold tubes that were woven into each hair tress, but stylized lotus blossoms were the preferred adornment for others. This preference for elaborate decoration later developed into the use of jewelry that was made of gold, turquoise, and other semiprecious stones or beads. When attending special banquets or festivities, wealthy women often tied cones of scented animal fat, called perfume pomades, to their wigs. The fat would melt in the Egyptian sun and slide down the wig, emitting a pleasant smell as it did so.

Wealthy women relied on female servants to apply their wigs and adorn them with the proper decorations. The servants were also responsible for the upkeep of the wigs. The wigs were washed, brushed, and scented on a daily basis and were kept fresh for the owner's use. When not in use, the hairpieces were kept in special boxes. Since it was believed that wigs would be needed in the afterlife, the rich were always buried with several of their wigs. Many of these were found thousands of years later by archaeologists in Egyptian tombs.

Wealthy Women and Their Jewelry

Ancient Egyptian women also valued personal adornment and wore jewelry of every size and description. Wealthy women took great pride in their jewelry and used bracelets, necklaces, and earrings to enhance their appearance. Like other aspects of their appearance, women used jewelry to improve their beauty and prestige in Egyptian society.

Necklaces came in a wide variety of styles, including chokers, single– and multiple–strand necklaces, pendants, and broad collars. The most characteristic Egyptian necklace was the broad collar which could measure up to ten inches wide and consisted of multiple strands of beads, tubes, or stone figures. Among the most impressive and elegant jewelry are some of the pendants and necklaces found in the tombs of wealthy Egyptian women and royal princesses. Their jewelry was primarily made of gold, with inlays of semiprecious turquoise, lapis lazuli, garnet, carnelian, and other stones.

Wealthy Egyptian women wore fine jewelry as a symbol of their privileged status. Here, a group of ornately jeweled women dine at a banquet.

Historians have learned a great deal about Egyptian jewelry from what archaeologists have discovered in the tombs and vaults of various rich women. During one excavation archaeologist and historian Zahi Hawass uncovered the tomb of a wealthy woman named Naes, who apparently was the wife of a governor. Hawass describes some of his findings: "Most of her adornments and jewelry were intact. Her burial shroud was decorated with amulets of precious stone as well as at least eighty–four gold beads. Embalmers had replaced her tongue with a shield–shaped piece of gold."[16] Historians agree that the splendor and richness of her mortuary complex reflected the family's high standing in Egyptian society.

Wealthy Women at Leisure

With a household full of servants to see to her every need, a rich Egyptian woman had plenty of time for relaxation and leisure activities. In the late afternoon, for instance, a wealthy woman and her family often sat under the awning of their villa relaxing, drinking wine, and listening to a variety of music being played by hired musicians. She and her husband would talk of the day they had just spent and plan future festivities and outings. Their children would play nearby, supervised by a nanny or children's servant.

On the days when her husband did not work, a rich woman and her children often accompanied him on a variety of excursions, such as an outing on the river and marshes of Egypt. The Nile was often alive with boats, barges, and crafts of all kinds carrying other wealthy families for a day's outing. Tomb paintings depict numerous wealthy women sailing on the river with their families during such excursions. The boat, made of either papyrus reeds or wood, would often have a canopy or covering to shade the woman, who usually was seated in the back of the boat while oarsmen rowed and tended the sails.

Wealthy women also accompanied their husbands when they went hunting. Historian Breasted describes such an out-

Other Leisure Activities

Wealthy women had a lot of time to relax and enjoy themselves, and so they played many games. Women often enjoyed a game called "dogs and jackals." This game has been found in the tombs of many wealthy Egyptian women. Its board was made of wood, ebony, or ivory and was shaped somewhat like a small piece of furniture. It had four legs carved in the shapes of animals. The board itself contained fifty-five holes. There were also drawers that held ebony pawns; the pawns were mounted on sticks and were shaped like the heads of jackals and dogs. Three coins were used to determine the movement of the pieces on the board. The first person with all the pieces won the game.

In addition to board games, wealthy women attended a variety of sporting contests. They particularly enjoyed wrestling and javelin-throwing events. Women dressed in their finest clothing to attend these sporting competitions and cheered loudly for their favorite athletes. These events, along with the large numbers of patrons watching the contests, are depicted in numerous tomb paintings and engravings.

In this wall painting, Queen Nefertiti plays Senet, *a board game similar to Chinese checkers that was very popular with the ancient Egyptians.*

ing: "While the lady plucked water–lilies and lotus flowers . . . [her husband] launched his boomerang among the flocks of wild fowl."[17] This type of trip was not a primitive camping venture but rather an elaborate excursion made with the finest of foods and accommodations, all provided by a retinue of servants and assistants.

In addition to such outings with her family, wealthy women also enjoyed a variety of games played with her husband or other members of her family. The most popular of these games was *Senet*, which was played by two people. The board game consisted of thirty squares in which a wooden or bone lion and an antelope pitted their wits against each other. It was similar to Chinese checkers: Each player tried to cross the board while blocking the advance of his or her opponent. The board, made of wood, ebony, or stone, had many squares that were marked with hazards such as "water" or "fire," but other squares represented advantages such as "beauty" or "power." The moves were made according to the way that small pieces of wood landed when thrown (similar to dice). "Completing the game," historian Silverman explains, "was equated with successfully passing divine judgment of the soul and being reborn in the afterlife."[18] For the Egyptians, the game represented a struggle against the forces of evil that in real life might prevent one from reaching the afterlife. This board game was often placed in the tombs of the wealthy so that they would have entertainment when they reached the afterlife.

Whether maintaining the elegance of their own homes or entertaining others, wealthy women played a variety of important roles in Egyptian society. By enhancing their appearance and beauty, rich women were seen as the epitome of what was desirable in all Egyptian women.

Chapter 3: Women and Religion

For the ancient Egyptians, religion was a tolerant, all–encompassing belief system that was practiced by all social classes and genders. The central tenet of their religion held that the world had been created out of nothingness and that, if the proper religious rituals were not followed, chaos and darkness would return. The Egyptians believed that it was possible to alter the world around them by directing the unseen forces of gods and spirits. Historians Bob Brier and Hoyt Hobbs stress the importance of these beliefs: "Nothing affected the everyday life of ancient Egyptians more than their religion."[19]

As in every other facet of Egyptian life, women played a crucial role in the religious and spiritual life of the family, the community, and the empire. Egyptian women of all classes were responsible for assuring that their households contained religious objects dedicated to the gods and goddesses. In addition to praying to the deities, the ancient Egyptians worshipped their ancestors: Women were responsible for the upkeep of ancestor shrines and led the family in worship and prayer on a daily basis.

Women were responsible for ensuring that the ancestors and gods were honored and given offerings. They were also actively involved in all funerals, often planning the rituals and overseeing that the proper ceremonies were performed. Many women of the royalty and nobility served as priestesses in the numerous temples that were located throughout Egypt, and others were professional mourners at funerals.

Female Magicians

Magic and superstitious beliefs played a large role in the Egyptian religion. The ancient Egyptians believed that through magical powers called *heka* they could influence deities and ancestors to work on their behalf. There were thousands of professional magicians, many of whom were women. They traveled throughout the empire performing feats of magic while selling magic charms and spells.

An Egyptian woman (right) holds an ankh, a prevalent symbol of long life in ancient Egypt.

These women traveled with other magicians, read palms, predicted the future, and advised their clients to obtain certain spells and charms to protect them from harm. Numerous pharaohs employed female magicians to predict the outcomes of battles and to warn of impending invasions, droughts, or disasters. Pharaohs also consulted female magicians to protect themselves and their families from the evil spirits that all Egyptians believed inhabited their world.

Female magicians also advised their clients on the need to wear amulets and charms to repel harmful forces or to endow the wearer with good luck. For example, if the magician saw danger ahead for her client, she prescribed red amulets; meanwhile, blue or green charms were suggested for someone to achieve growth and good health. Historian Rosalie David explains that amulets and charms protected "the wearer against a range of hostile forces and events, which included ferocious animals, disease, famine, accidents, and natural disasters."[20]

Female magicians sold a wide variety of magic charms and amulets to their clients. Many of these took the form of popular gods, ritual objects, animals, plants, and body parts, but others were engraved with the names of former kings. The ankh, a cross with a loop at the top, was worn by nearly everyone to ensure a long life. The scarab beetle was another popular charm and was believed to symbolize the sun at dawn, a potent sign of rebirth. The Egyptians believed that such amulets would bring them luck, good health, and success.

Magical Spells and Potions

Egyptian women played a significant role in the application of magical spells and potions, many of which were employed at important times of life, such as marriage, death, and childbirth. It was very important, for instance, that childbirth be accompanied by specific magic spells lest a child

The Sun God and Creation

The ancient Egyptians believed that the world was in darkness and chaos at the beginning of time. At some point the sun god, Re, they believed, gave birth to himself and became the supreme deity and the ancestor of all future pharaohs. The sun god was the dominant deity in Egyptian religion, although he took many different forms and names. It was believed that from Re's tears came the first Egyptian people.

Re created Shu, the god of air; and Tefnut, the goddess of moisture. Their children, in turn, were Geb, the god of the Earth; and Nut, the goddess of the sky. Nut and Geb also had children: Isis, Osiris, Seth (Set), and Nepthys. According to Egyptian myth, at the birth of Osiris a voice was heard throughout the land proclaiming that the lord of all the earth had been born. Later Osiris became the king of Egypt while Isis ruled as his queen. He was believed to have established laws and then taught the Egyptians how to grow food and how to worship the gods.

Osiris had one enemy—his brother, Seth. Jealous of his brother's power, Seth killed Osiris, tearing his body into pieces and scattering them all over Egypt. Isis traveled all over Egypt gathering up her husband's pieces. She eventually put him together long enough to conceive a child. At that point, Osiris went to live and rule over the world of the dead. Meanwhile, Isis gave birth to Horus, who became the rightful king of Egypt and took revenge on Seth. The Egyptians saw in this struggle the classic fight between good and evil.

The ancient Egyptians worshipped the sun god Re (left) as their supreme deity.

be born under the influence of evil spirits. For these reasons, collections of spells were treasured possessions and typically were handed down from mothers to daughters.

Women of every class used these spells to protect their families from harm. Before her family went to bed at night, for example, a woman chanted spells to guard her sleeping family, to drive away scorpions, and to prevent nightmares. She mixed and used potions on potential suitors for herself or her children to enhance love, to keep her family from being eaten by crocodiles and other animals, and to protect her husband when he traveled to foreign lands. Women also utilized magic when burying a loved one: They often chanted a special spell to prevent their family members from entering the afterworld upside down. Unless the deceased were upright, there was no chance for them to reach perfection and happiness in heaven.

Women and the Goddess Isis

The ancient Egyptians believed that the gods and goddesses were the only forces that could maintain the balance of order in the universe. For this reason, they were honored, revered, and worshipped by everyone. As the early Egyptians formed settlements, local deities emerged and played a significant role in everyday life. Historians, in fact, estimate that there were around two thousand different gods and goddesses who were worshipped in ancient Egypt. These deities, the Egyptians believed, controlled every aspect of nature and daily life.

Although they prayed to many gods, Egyptian women primarily worshipped a few goddesses on a daily basis. The most enduringly popular of all goddesses was Isis, the symbol of the Egyptian wife and mother. Her significance to Egyptian women is detailed by historian Betina Knapp: "Isis, great mother goddess of the Egyptians, was worshipped not only for her protective, healing, nutritive, loving, and compassionate qualities, but for her strength, initiative, independence, and rational approach to life."[21] Numerous depictions of Isis have survived on tomb paintings, sculptures, and temple walls. Many of these show the goddess tenderly nursing her son, and others show the tears she shed following her husband's death.

An Egyptian woman prayed to Isis to help her became a good wife and mother and to help her nurture and care for her family. Women of all classes kept small statues and other depictions of Isis in their homes. They also worshipped the goddess at the many temples dedicated to her throughout Egypt. Isis was worshipped for over three thousand years, not only by the Egyptians but by many other cultures as well. The goddess's appeal spread throughout the ancient world, with a large following in Greece and the Roman Empire. The cult of Isis, the Greeks and Romans both believed, offered personal salvation for the soul. Isis became the ideal woman: She was nurturing yet fierce to defend those she loved. Historian Joann Fletcher summarizes Isis's importance to women: "Isis was a goddess of enormous magical powers and was said to be more powerful than a thousand soldiers and more clever than a million gods."[22]

Hathor and Bastet

In addition to worshipping Isis, Egyptian women also prayed to two other goddesses for support and wisdom: Hathor and Bastet. Statues of both goddesses adorned many Egyptian homes.

Hathor was worshipped as a great mother who was usually seen nursing an infant pharaoh. Her smile was also believed to give kings long life and great power. Hathor's significance to the women of Egypt is summarized by historian David Silverman: "Because Hathor was closely connected with sexuality, fertility, pregnancy, and childbirth, she was a particularly important deity for women, many of whom undoubtedly visited her

Isis was the most popular Egyptian goddess. Women worshipped her as the mother of all Egyptians.

shrines with gifts and petitions."[23] Many temples were dedicated in Hathor's honor, and a large group of priestesses was associated with this important goddess.

Hathor's primary temple was at Dendera in Upper Egypt, where she was worshipped by thousands of Egyptian women. A large retinue of priestesses served the goddess within the temple and ministered to the women who came to worship. One of the most important feast days in ancient Egypt, in fact, was dedicated to this goddess. During this festival, Hathor's statue was taken from her shrine at Dendera and presented to the people. Accompanied by a group of priestesses and female musicians and dancers, the entire local population often turned out for this festival and enjoyed several days of music and other entertainment in celebration of the goddess's good works.

Egyptian women also revered Bastet the cat–headed goddess, for her fertility. Women who wanted children often prayed to Bastet, who was usually depicted as a cat with a litter of kittens at her side. Bastet was worshipped as the guardian of all cats, animals who were sacred and beloved in ancient Egypt. Bastet was also depicted as the sun's power to ripen crops. During the New Year holiday, women gave each other amulets of Bastet as presents to bring good luck and pregnancy.

Priestesses

Hundreds, if not thousands, of Egyptian women served as priestesses in Egyptian temples. Doing so was regarded as an honor, not a job. Not only were priestesses highly regarded members of Egyptian society during their lifetimes but many could also expect further praise and honor in the afterlife. Most priestesses came from high–ranking families. Priestesses played a key role in Egyptian religion and life, for they were the people responsible for keeping the gods and goddesses happy.

A priestess began her day with her servants dressing and bathing her before sunrise. Male servants carried her to the temple on a small platform, clearing a path by making people step aside as she passed. Prior to entering any part of the temple, a priestess had to purify herself by dressing in special robes and flowing gowns. She often sprinkled herself with incense–flavored scents that would appeal to the deities. Once attired and scented in the proper manner, the priestess entered the temple to perform her sacred duties.

Priestesses were responsible for a variety of tasks in the temples. While they chanted prayers, sang sacred hymns, and played musical instruments, their most important task was to simply honor the goddess for whom the temple was built. To accomplish this, they looked after the temple statues; made offerings of flowers,

Many women served as priestesses like those depicted here. Priestesses were highly respected members of Egyptian society.

incense, food, and drink; and supervised temple servants and temple estates.

Each day ceremonies were held to honor the goddess of the temple. The priestesses' first task was to awaken the deity, a task that was accomplished by a procession of priestesses, all singing and chanting as they entered the goddess's sanctuary. The priestesses then made offerings of food and drink to the deity, for the ancient Egyptians believed that the gods needed nourishment. Following this, the statue of the goddess was washed and dressed in fresh clothes, just as if the figure were alive. Water was sprinkled around the statue, flowers and perfume were provided, and the outer door to the sanctuary was sealed. Incense was

A group of women at a funeral mourns the death of a loved one. Women performed a number of funerary rites designed to assist loved ones on their journey to the afterlife.

burned to attract the attention of the goddess. All of these tasks were believed to encourage the deity's spirit to live and remain in the temple, thus bringing protection to the entire community.

Temple Musicians

Ancient Egyptian priestesses were also responsible for providing music to entertain the goddess. Many priestesses carried a sacred rattle known as a *sistrum*. They used this instrument together with a special necklace called a *menat*. Both were linked to the cult of the goddess Hathor, who was known for her fondness of music and dance. The *sistrum*, in fact, had a handle shaped like the head of Hathor. The Egyptians believed music and dancing gave pleasure to the deity, further ensuring that she would be benevolent to her worshippers.

In addition to the various priestesses, other Egyptian women (usually wealthy ones) worked at the temples and served as the songstress, dancer, or musician of a specific goddess. The Egyptians believed that music was an important way of communicating with the deities, and the women who held these positions were regarded as instrumental in soothing and satisfying the goddesses' desires. Because of their important work, they were greatly respected by other Egyptians. Some of these women also worked alongside male priests in those Egyptian temples dedicated to the gods.

Music of every sort was used to accompany temple rituals. Women sang, danced, and played instruments during prayers and also during the dressing and feeding of the deities. Many musicians and dancers also played at festivals celebrating the gods and goddesses.

Historians have been able to learn a great deal about such women from tomb depictions and other art forms. Archaeologists, for instance, uncovered a scene from Pharaoh Hatshepsut's Karnak Temple that shows a group of women singing. The women are clad in flowing white robes, have flowers in their hair, and are singing and dancing outside the temple. Their faces are joyful as they perform songs of adulation and praise.

God's Wife of Amun

During the New Kingdom (1555 to 712 B.C.) one of the most important religious positions held by a woman was that of the god's wife of Amun. The wife, sister, or daughter of the reigning pharaoh usually held this position. The ancient Egyptians believed that the pharaoh and his wife and other family members were directly descended from the gods and, therefore, were semidivine. This belief in the divinity of rulers and their wives gave legitimacy and great significance to the position of god's wife.

The god's wife was responsible for taking part in special ceremonies at the

Temple of Amun in Karnak. These ceremonies were held to bring fertility and prosperity to Egypt. As god's wife, an Egyptian queen or princess was expected to carry out rituals before the statue of Amun, the sun god. She accomplished this by shaking a *sistrum* in order to stimulate the deity. This was believed to maintain the created world and bring success to the empire. In addition to her role at the temple, the god's wife controlled vast estates and held considerable political power.

The role of god's wife had its origins at the beginning of the New Kingdom, when the title was bestowed by Pharaoh Ahmose on his queen, Ahmose Nefertair. Several queens later used this position of importance to gain control and power over large parts of the government. Hatshepsut was perhaps the most notable god's wife of Amun. While serving in this position, Hatshepsut acquired a powerful group of advisers and allies, whom she later used to secure the throne. After serving as pharaoh for twenty years, Hatshepsut's death saw the decline of the god's wife position and its eventual elimination.

Women and the Afterlife

While some women served in special religious roles, all Egyptian women expected to share the same afterlife as men. The afterlife was believed to be a place where there was neither illness nor famine. It was a place where crops grew to a great height and where harvesting was an easy task to be performed in one's finest clothes without fear of getting dirty. The afterlife, the ancient Egyptians believed, was filled with riches and bountiful food, an improvement in every way on their earthly lives. Women further believed that after death their youthful beauty would be restored and that they would remain an ageless beauty for eternity.

Ancient Egyptian women believed that every human being had spiritual elements that survived death. One spiritual element was known as *ka*, which they believed was a woman's life force. The *ka* needed nourishment in the afterlife to survive. Another spiritual element, known as a *ba*, held a woman's memory and personality. After death, Egyptian women believed that the *ba* made a dangerous journey through the underworld to a place where the dead were judged. The Egyptians called this underworld *duat* and believed that parts of it were full of perils such as snakes and fire. To achieve peace and a happy eternity, a person's soul had to pass through these dangers.

Egyptian women believed that once their souls, or the souls of their ancestors, had passed safely through the dangers of the afterworld, they would become powerful spirits, or *akhs*. At this point they could expect to have life everlasting in a

Mummification

The Egyptians believed that the preservation of the corpse was fundamental to enabling life after death. As their society developed, they became experts in a process of burial called mummification, which preserved the body by drying it.

The entire process of mummification usually took seventy days to complete. Following death, the body was taken to a group of embalmers. These specialists removed the liver, brain, and lungs; dried them; and stored them in special vessels called canopic jars. The heart was the only organ left in the body during the embalming process. After the embalmers removed the organs, they covered the body with natron, a substance that not only dried the body but also kept it from decaying. Natron crystals were packed all around the corpse, and within forty to seventy days the body would be ready for the final stages of burial. The body was wrapped in linen and placed in a coffin or a sarcophagus which was taken to the tomb for proper burial.

It is the process of mummification that has allowed archaeologists to learn so much about the history of ancient Egypt. Some of the bodies that have been excavated are in such good condition that medical researchers have been able to determine the cause of death five thousand years later.

land of fertile fields called the Fields of Yaru. Egyptian women prayed for such an afterlife for themselves and their loved ones and expected that everyone would live in happiness for all eternity. This could only happen, however, if the souls of the dead were properly honored and respected through the use of specific funerary rites, including a proper burial.

Funerary Rites

When their family members died, Egyptian women chanted spells to ensure that their loved ones had a safe journey to the afterlife. The spells, women hoped, would counteract many of the dangers their loved ones would face. Many of these spells were written on the outsides of the coffins and sarcophagi. *National Geographic* journalist Kent R. Weeks explains the purpose of such writings: "For the Egyptians, the plan of a tomb was like a road map from this world to the next. . . . The tomb's decorations were like a guidebook."[24] Eventually many of these spells, along with a map of the underworld, were put on ornate scrolls and placed in a book that is now known as the *Book of the Dead.* This book was used by all Egyptians to properly prepare the dead for burial and safe passage.

Following the death of a loved one, Egyptian women were responsible for preparing the body for a proper burial. It was essential, that the women treated the bodies of their loved ones with the utmost respect. Women generally relied on information that had been passed down by their mothers and grandmothers or the guidelines outlined in the *Book of the Dead*. An excerpt from the book describes what is required for a body to be accepted into the afterlife: "[The dead have to be] pure, clean, clothed in fresh linen and anointed with the finest myrrh oil."[25]

Wealthy women and women of royalty relied on their servants to prepare the body of a loved one before it was sent on to the professionals who specialized in mummification, a process that preserved the corpse. Peasant women, on the other hand, prepared the body themselves for burial. These women bathed their deceased loved ones with water and a combination of fragrant oils before dressing them in their finest clothing. Great care was taken in selecting an appropriate wig or hairstyle for the important journey to the afterlife. Peasant families could not afford elaborate funeral rites or coffins, so deceased family members were often wrapped in linen and then buried in small family cemeteries or in the nearby desert.

The actual funeral procession was well planned and carried out by the surviving spouse or children of the deceased. Peasants usually carried their dead family members to the burial site, but those who could afford caskets used an ox–drawn cart. Family members from all classes walked behind the body toward the burial site. Egyptian women generally wore headbands of blue cloth, signifying the loss of a loved one.

Professional Mourners

A group of female mourners, all weeping and grieving, walked behind the family to the graveside. These mourners were generally considered professional in that they had no relation to the family. They were paid with offerings of food and other goods, and they were a common feature of funerals in small villages and communities. Tomb paintings depict professional mourners following the casket, pulling their hair and visibly mourning the family's loss of a loved one. Historian Silverman describes their appearance: "Their hair is disheveled, their breasts bared, and tears spill from their eyes."[26] Professional women mourners danced and sang at the graveside in honor of the goddess Hathor, who the Egyptians believed could help the dead be reborn into the afterlife. The noise of music and dancing was also believed to reactivate the hearing and sight of the dead,

Female mourners play tambourines and dance during a funeral procession. The noise of the music was thought to awaken the senses of hearing and sight in the dead.

enabling them to see and hear during their journey to the afterlife.

In addition to the professional mourners, two women from the deceased person's family were often selected to portray the roles of the goddesses Isis and Nephthys. According to Egyptian myth, Isis and Nephthys mourned for the dead god Osiris. They searched Egypt for the pieces of Osiris's dismembered body and then put him back together again. By portraying these two goddesses at the funeral, the Egyptians believed the deceased would more easily find new life.

The actual burial took many forms. Peasants and others, being unable to afford elaborate tombs and the services of priests, performed all the burial rituals themselves. Peasant women often led the praying, and female friends and family took charge of burying some of the deceased's prized belongings. Each family member helped dig the grave and then refill it after the body had been lowered into the ground. The wealthy class used the services of a vast fleet of professionals to put on a much more elaborate burial ceremony.

After the Funeral

Female family members of the peasant class were in charge of preparing a lush feast after the burial ceremony, while rich women employed hundreds of servants to feed and serve the guests. The relative wealth of the family was a decisive factor in the amount and type of food served. Peasant women prepared dozens of loaves of bread, numerous fruits and vegetables, and whatever meat, fowl, or fish was available in their community. Beer was the beverage of choice, prepared ahead of time by female family members. The wealthy served the same kinds of food but added beef, imported fruits, wine, and exotic vegetables to the menu. These kinds of meals and the accompa-

Wealthy Egyptians were laid to rest in elaborately decorated tombs like this one. It was the responsibility of women to maintain these tombs.

nying festivities could last anywhere from two to five days.

Egyptian women participated in many after–death rituals and ceremonies. After an ancestor's death, for instance, it was the responsibility of the family to maintain the tomb and make the necessary offerings and prayers to ensure the continued goodwill of the deceased. Many tomb depictions show female family members playing a prominent role in these rituals. Women are shown burning incense, pouring drinks for the dead, and dedicating various offerings of flowers, food, and drink. In the absence of a male survivor, women took the primary role for overseeing that the ancestor was properly respected and the grave sites were properly maintained.

Believing that the living could maintain contact and communicate with the dead, many Egyptian women wrote letters to their deceased husbands. Some of these letters were placed within the tomb to accompany the person on the journey to the afterlife. Others were written following the burial ceremony and were left in the tomb vault or near the grave along with other offerings. The editors of Time–Life Books explain the content of such letters: "Some of these letters seem merely conversational, asking advice about daily problems. Others beseech and implore, requesting assistance with family illnesses and financial matters."[27] Egyptian women fully expected their ancestors to answer their prayers by protecting the family and making their lives better.

Religion and the belief in the power of the deities influenced every aspect of ancient Egyptian life. As in other areas of Egyptian society, women played significant roles in nearly all facets of religious life. Their faith, along with their belief in and knowledge of magic, would carry over into a variety of other professions and tasks.

Chapter 4: Women in Medicine

Medicine in ancient Egypt was but one aspect of a very advanced civilization. Unlike other early civilizations that utilized medicine men or shamans to treat disease, the Egyptians made use of a highly trained group of physicians. Egypt, in fact, was one of the first civilizations in the world to have trained doctors who treated illnesses and performed surgeries. Homer, a ninth–century B.C. Greek poet, verified this fact in one of his many writings: "In medical knowledge, the Egyptian leaves the rest of the world behind."[28]

The field of medicine was open to women from the earliest times of ancient Egyptian history. For thousands of years female physicians, healers, and midwives played crucial roles in the treatment of many illnesses. Female physicians underwent the same kind of extensive training that their male counterparts did and worked in every field of medical specialty. Other Egyptian women, while not physicians, played an active role in medicine by serving as temple healers, nurses, masseuses, and midwives.

Historians have been able to learn a great deal about Egyptian medicine from the discovery of several important documents. The oldest of these, the Kahun Gynecology Papyrus, dates back to 1825 B.C. It describes various methods of diagnosing pregnancy and includes ways of promoting fertility and treating many gynecological illnesses. Two other documents have added a wealth of information to what scholars know about this topic. The Edwin Smith Papyrus (1600 B.C.), for example, is chiefly concerned with surgery and describes nearly fifty surgical cases and how they were treated; meanwhile, the Ebers Papyrus (1500 B.C.) outlines treatment for chest pain and a variety of other diseases. These papers have given historians a valuable glimpse into the practice of medicine in ancient Egypt.

Female Doctors

There were more than one hundred documented female physicians, and likely hundreds of others, who practiced medicine in ancient Egypt. Peseshet was the

This wooden panel depicts Hesire, a famous physician in ancient Egypt. The field of medicine was open to women from the earliest years of Egyptian history.

first female doctor in the world and worked during the time of the great pyramids, sometime between 3200 and 2300 B.C. She was given the honorary title Lady Overseer of the Lady Physicians, and, as such, trained and then supervised a group of female doctors. She also taught midwives at the medical school of Sais and was director of the soul–priestesses, a group of women who supervised many Egyptian funerary cults. Little information has survived about these women.

To learn their skills, women attended medical schools, where they were taught by highly trained professional physicians, many of whom were female. Many of these schools were located at various temples scattered throughout Egypt. These medical schools were perhaps Egypt's greatest bequest to future generations.

The most famous school was located in Memphis, where Egypt's premier physician, Imhotep, taught thousands of medical students. In these schools, women were taught by practicing physicians, midwives, and other healers. They learned how to treat hundreds of illnesses, how to perform simple surgeries, and what herbs and medicines to prescribe for patients. They also had to learn human anatomy, organ function, the location of the heart and brain, and bone structure. Upon graduation, female physicians took an oath similar to the one that doctors take today, vowing not to do anything that harmed a patient. Other women with medical skills were trained by family members who knew medicine, and still others served as apprentices to trained female physicians.

"Some Treat the Eye, Some the Teeth"

Most female Egyptian doctors specialized in only one kind of medicine. Herodotus, a Greek historian who wrote during the fifth century B.C., addressed this specialization: "The practice of medicine is very specialized among them. Each physician treats just one disease. The country is full of physicians, some treat the eye, some the teeth, some of what belongs to the abdomen, and others internal diseases."[29] Specialization enabled female doctors to provide the best care to a variety of patients.

Most of the women who became doctors specialized in the treatment of other women: They became experts in the obstetrical and gynecological fields of medicine. They surgically delivered babies and also undertook complicated gynecological procedures, including the surgical removal of cancerous breasts and other organs.

Although most women served in these specialized fields, some female doctors had general practices in the villages and towns of ancient Egypt. Today they would be called family practitioners. Many wealthy women with medical skills, for example, saw patients in sepa-

Female Dentists

In addition to serving as physicians, many Egyptian women became dentists. Like medical practitioners, dentists were highly trained to work on the mouth, teeth, and gums. Numerous documents have survived that describe various dental treatments such as tooth extraction, the treatment of mouth ulcers, and jaw dislocations.

The most common procedure that women dentists performed was the draining of an abscessed tooth. Using a scalpel and a sharpened dental pick made of bone, the dentist surgically opened a hole in the infected tooth and drained the infection. Dentists also filled cavities with a concoction made of resin and chrysocolla, a copperlike mineral. Female dentists also treated loose teeth by connecting them to sturdy teeth with wire bridges.

Remains of such dental work were discovered in recovered mummies of the period. One mummy, in fact, had three substitute teeth skillfully tied to the other teeth with gold wire.

rate facilities on their estates and provided medical care to their employees. Others served in the communities, often going door to door to offer relief for a wide variety of ailments.

Advanced Medical Care

Patients of female physicians in Egypt often recovered from their illnesses. Modern–day physicians have found extensive proof of their ancient counterparts' successes by examining preserved Egyptian mummies. Scientists, for instance, have discovered hundreds of healed fractures and wounds, extensive dental surgeries, as well as at least one case of successful brain surgery. From these modern examinations, scientists have determined that female physicians were very knowledgeable about the human body and quite successful in many of their treatments.

In general, female physicians kept good records of their patients and their problems. The discovery of many of these documents has added to the knowledge that modern scholars have about ancient Egyptian medicine. Female doctors apparently knew of the importance of diet and had an extensive knowledge of natural drugs. They practiced holistic medicine, a kind of medicine that involved not only taking care of a person's physical symptoms, but also treating their spiritual, emotional, and social needs.

Medical Treatment

Female physicians saw both male and female patients who needed treatment for a variety of diseases. Smallpox, bubonic plague, malaria, measles, tuberculosis, and cholera were all prevalent in ancient Egypt. Many of these illnesses were difficult to cure, however, and resulted in large numbers of deaths. Even smaller problems such as diarrhea or cuts could often prove fatal if not treated properly. Arthritis, rheumatism, cancer, and respiratory illnesses were also common. Surviving documents attest to the presence of these diseases and outline the treatment of such maladies.

Most patients were examined and treated in their homes. Female doctors performed much the same kind of examination that is done today. Before the actual physical examination took place, the Egyptian doctor interviewed her patient to learn about the symptoms of the particular ailment. Patients were asked about their daily life habits and their diet. Because the ancient Egyptians believed that most disease was caused by angry spirits, female physicians asked their patients if they had any enemies or had done anything to anger another person or a god. Once these questions had been answered, the physician examined her patient. She took her patient's pulse, examined the skin, and checked the abdomen and other parts of the body for swelling and pain. After these steps, the doctor arrived at a diagnosis and a treatment plan.

Many Egyptian physicians were assisted by women who served as nurses. Nurses were generally trained by the doctors who employed them. Female nurses learned basic anatomy and physiology, an overview of Egyptian health problems, and simple nursing procedures. Nurses helped the doctors during the physical examination and often were responsible for teaching patients how to care for wounds and other problems. A number of women were also hired by the wealthy to provide hands–on care to ailing family members.

Specific Treatment

After giving their patients a thorough examination, female physicians recommended a variety of treatments. Women doctors might have suggested heliotherapy, or exposure to ultraviolet sun rays, as a way to ease their patients' pain. The ancient Egyptians believed that the sun's rays had the power to heal. While the Egyptians did not understand the exact mechanism by which the sun provided healing, they documented its effectiveness in improving the health of their patients. Modern physicians now know that the sun indeed provides healing vitamins and minerals that contribute to better health.

Physiotherapy might also be used; many physicians and female masseuses are depicted in tomb paintings massaging a patient's muscles to relieve pain and soreness. Hundreds of Egyptian women were trained in the art of massage in special schools run by female physicians. Female masseuses were taught to use aromatic herbs and oils to massage tight muscles to relieve pain. Many of these therapies were used in combination to treat a variety of ills.

Most female physicians used herbal therapy as the primary method of treatment for their patients. Herbal remedies were prescribed for a variety of illnesses and were often quite effective; many of the same medicinal herbs used in ancient Egypt are still in use today throughout the world. The most common herbs used by female doctors were garlic, onion, senna, sycamore, castor oil, acacia gum, mint, and linseed. They also used yeast. Female physicians often told their patients to swallow yeast to help with indigestion. They also prescribed it to cure leg ulcers and other wounds. They used castor oil combined with figs and dates to help

Prescriptions for Disease and Injuries

Women physicians treated hundreds of different diseases in ancient Egypt. As healers, these doctors could prescribe medications in the form of pills, cakes, salves, drops, gargles, suppositories, fumigations, and baths. While some of the remedies that were given seem archaic and even repulsive today, scientists admit that many of the formulas did work. Many of these medicines actually relied on their repulsiveness to be effective. The Egyptians believed that the spirits that caused disease would be repelled by the smells. As a result, turtle brains, lizard blood, and the urine of virgins were all popular remedies.

Women physicians ordered many different prescriptions and remedies. A cure for diarrhea, for instance, consisted of one-eighth cup of figs and grapes, bread dough, pit corn, fresh earth, onion, and elderberry. The patient drank this mixture. Indigestion was treated by telling the patient to crush a hog's tooth and put it inside four sugar cakes, which were then eaten for four days. Burns were treated by mixing the breast milk of a woman who had given birth to a male child with gum and a ram's hair. According to Egyptian historians cited on the EMuseum Web site of Minnesota State University at Mankato, the person or family was told to say, "Thy son Horus is burnt in the desert. Is there any water there? There is no water. I have water in my mouth . . . [and] have come to extinguish the fire."

relieve constipation and chose cloves of garlic to treat everyday ills, such as an upset stomach and the common cold.

Female doctors were frequently called on to treat asthma, a disease that was prevalent in ancient Egypt and worsened by the constantly blowing sand. They used an early form of inhalation therapy that was quite effective in treating this disease. A mixture of honey, cream, milk, garlic, and date kernels was prepared, heated, and the fumes were inhaled by the patient. The Ebers Papyrus documents how the mixture was used:

> Bring seven stones and heat them on a fire. Take one of them, place parts of these drugs over it, cover it with a new jar with a pierced bottom. Introduce a tube of reed through this hole and put your mouth on this tube so that you swallow its fumes.[30]

Female doctors then instructed their patients to perform this procedure at home several times a day to ease their breathing problems.

Female physicians also treated wounds and cuts. After suturing a wound, the doctor applied raw meat to the area and told the patient to leave this in place for twenty–four hours. She instructed her patient to then replace the meat with a dressing made of astringent herbs, honey, butter, and moldy bread. Modern physicians have attested to the efficacy of such a treatment. Raw meat, scientists now know, can prevent bleeding, and honey stimulates the secretion of white blood cells, an important part of the healing process. The application of moldy bread remained the preferred method of treating wounds for hundreds of years, and in 1928 Alexander Fleming was successful in extracting the antibiotic penicillin from bread mold.

"Come Remedy!"

In order to treat their patients, female physicians relied on both medical practices and magic. Historian David Silverman elaborates: "The Egyptians believed that disease and misfortune derived from malign spirits and the hostile dead, and that maintaining health was a matter of providing protection against these forces."[31] Magic, therefore, was not an alternative to regular treatment but rather a complementary part of the total healing process. Hundreds of female physicians in ancient Egypt used spells and incantations, often targeted at the supernatural beings believed to be making a person sick. Egyptian historians recount one such spell that a female physician passed on to a patient: "Come Remedy! Come thou who expellest evil things in this my stomach and in these my limbs."[32]

In addition to treating the sick with medicine and magic, female physicians in ancient Egypt also performed surgery. These surgeons used a variety of surgical instruments, including scalpels, bone saws, scissors, copper needles, forceps, and probes. The scalpels used by female doctors had blades made of obsidian, a black stone that could be cut and filed to produce a sharp edge. According to ancient documents, the blades were heated and then used to make incisions. In addition to providing a clean cut, the heated blade sealed up blood vessels, limiting bleeding.

Women performed operations to heal a variety of conditions. They routinely removed cancerous breasts and other organs; mummies have been discovered with evidence of sutured wounds and other surgeries. One of the most common surgeries performed by female surgeons was the removal of a cyst or an abscess, which consisted of an inflammed pocket of pus under the skin. The Ebers Papyrus describes how surgeons should go about surgically removing a cyst: "Instructions for a swelling of pus. . . . A disease that I treat with knife treatment. If anything remains in pocket, it recurs."[33] To ensure comfort during surgery, female surgeons generally sedated their patients with opiates, but they could also administer local anesthesia when necessary. They prepared the anesthesia by mixing water with vinegar and pouring it over Memphite stone, a process that caused the mixture to give off carbon dioxide. Today, carbon dioxide is known for its local analgesic effect.

Gynecology and Obstetrics

The majority of female physicians in ancient Egypt specialized in the fields of medicine that related directly to female patients: obstetrics and gynecology. There were several medical schools devoted to training women in these two specialties. Women doctors were well trained, and ancient texts leave no doubt that these specialties were world renowned in ancient times. Both the ancient Greeks and Romans attest to the excellence and success of Egyptian obstetricians and gynecologists.

The treatment of female illnesses was especially important because Egyptian society emphasized fertility and childbearing. A woman's ability to conceive was of paramount importance, as historian Silverman explains: "The importance of women's reproductive role is reflected in the Egyptian's concern for female health and hygiene."[34] A number of medical scrolls deal specifically with the treatment and welfare of women and their offspring. These scrolls cover such topics as infertility, contraception, conception, pregnancy, miscarriage, childbirth, milk supply, and the well–being of infants. Other documents attest to the importance of prenatal care and the treatment of various gynecological problems and complications.

Women give birth with the aid of birthing stools in this carving. These stools were typically decorated with hieroglyphic prayers to the gods asking for a safe delivery.

Childbirth in ancient Egypt was dangerous for both the mother and the child. Infant mortality was especially high, over 30 percent at least, with the greatest danger coming prior to the age of five. Mortality, in fact, was so common that children were not regarded as full members of the community until they reached puberty. To minimize the risks associated with childbearing and birth, female physicians were well trained in the delivery process and in the immediate care of the newborn.

Female physicians had to recognize and treat various problems common to delivery. The Ebers Papyrus documents the treatment of one such problem—uterine bleeding:

> If you examine a woman who has had a discharge like water and the end of it is similar to baked blood, then you should say: This is a scrape in her uterus. Then you should make her: Nile earth from the water carrier, which you crush in honey and galena; put this on a dressing of fine linen and insert it into her vagina for four days.[35]

Female obstetricians also performed emergency surgery in the event that there were problems during the birth and delivery process. Surgery was often necessary if there was a breech birth, meaning the baby was coming out feet or bottom first. In these cases, female obstetricians attempted to manually turn the baby around in the birth canal. If this procedure was unsuccessful, the doctor opted to deliver the child through a surgery today known as a cesarean section. She would give the patient a mild anesthetic of some kind, then make an incision in the lower abdomen, and remove the baby in this manner. Using bone or stone needles, the obstetrician then tied off blood vessels with strong thread before closing the incision. The rate of success with this procedure was quite high among female physicians in ancient Egypt.

Treatment of Fertility Problems

Egyptian women were expected to get pregnant early in their marriages and have several children. Fertile women were considered successful and valuable. By becoming pregnant, Egyptian women gained the respect of their community and the approval of their husbands and families. Thus, it became imperative that any problems of conception be dealt with early in a woman's life. As a rule, women consulted female physicians to treat any and all fertility problems.

Many female physicians advised their infertile patients to mix beer and fresh dates with incense and then inhale the mixture as it burned over a fire. The vapors from this mixture were believed to improve the chances of getting pregnant. Other women were instructed to squat over a hot mix of frankincense, oil, dates, and beer and allow the vapors to enter their vaginas. The Egyptians believed this method removed any obstacle, physical or spiritual, that was preventing a pregnancy. A woman might also be advised to drink the breast milk of another woman who had recently borne a male child. Women who delivered boys were believed to be more fertile than women who delivered female children. The ancient Egyptians, while they valued all children, particularly sought male heirs who could carry on the professions of their fathers.

Many female physicians in ancient Egypt advised their patients to perform a simple fertility check to determine whether they were pregnant. Patients were instructed to pour their urine over two bags of seeds—one of wheat, the other of barley. The physician told the patient that if the seeds sprouted, it proved that she was

Egyptian physicians devised many ways to treat fertility problems, including the use of a variety of tonics and charms like this one.

pregnant. A positive result from the wheat meant the woman was going to have a boy; sprouting barley indicated a girl. This test continued to be used in Europe throughout the Middle Ages. Scientists today know that there are substances in a pregnant woman's urine that can cause grain to sprout or germinate, thus lending legitimacy to this ancient test.

Once a pregnancy was diagnosed, most Egyptian women continued to see their female physicians for several months. The doctor generally prescribed various herbs to take with meals and suggested prayers to various goddesses to assure a healthy child and a normal birth. Many female physicians also referred their patients to midwives, who would continue to monitor the pregnant woman and be present during the birth process.

The Role of the Midwife

Midwifery was an all–female profession in ancient Egypt. Midwives were trained in various ways and came from all walks of life. The midwife attending to a peasant woman, for instance, was usually a friend, neighbor, or family member who had previous experience with the delivery process. For the wealthy and royalty, the midwife was generally a trained maidservant or nurse who already lived in the household. Other pregnant women might go to various temples where experienced midwives ran small hospital–like operations devoted solely to the birth process.

The majority of Egyptian midwives had no formal training. Instead, they learned through apprenticeships in which knowledge was passed from family member to family member or from one practitioner to another. Other midwives, however, were so highly skilled that they taught female medical students how to be obstetricians and opened special schools to train women to become midwives.

The midwife had many responsibilities during the birth process. These included emotionally supporting and encouraging the mother, providing whatever medical care was needed, and offering spiritual and religious guidance. Midwives also used prescriptions to relieve any pain that accompanied labor and delivery. In cases of prolonged and difficult labor, for instance, the midwife could give the patient a mix of herbal remedies to soothe her pain.

In addition to prescribing oral remedies, Egyptian midwives used salves, ointments, and douches to facilitate delivery. To induce labor, for instance, midwives rubbed a woman's abdomen with a plaster of sea salt, emmer wheat, and plants such as rushes from the Nile River, a remedy believed to cause the uterus to contract and hasten labor. Another ancient prescription that helped induce labor was a mixture of the *kheper–wer* plant, honey, water of carob, and milk. The mixture was strained and placed directly in the uterus. Midwives might also seat the patient on warmed stones and then massage the abdomen in order to relax the uterus and induce delivery. A dish of hot water could also be placed under the birthing chair so that steam would help ease the pain of delivery.

Midwives advised pregnant women in ancient Egypt to use birthing stools during the delivery of their children. Birthing stools were small seats with a central hole on which the woman squatted to give birth. Midwives hired by the wealthy often used a specially designed wooden birthing chair equipped with a semicircular seat with two upright rods that the mother could grasp for support while bearing down during labor. Most of these chairs were decorated with hieroglyphic inscriptions, including written prayers to the gods and goddesses associated with birth.

Midwives and female family members who assisted with the birth of peasant babies usually recommended birthing bricks instead of expensive stools and chairs for use in labor and delivery. The midwife advised peasant women to kneel on the bricks, many of which were intricately decorated with painted scenes of goddesses and women giving birth. In many cases, these bricks, about fourteen inches long and seven inches wide, were passed on from family to family within the community.

During birth, the midwife positioned herself in front of the mother to help with the delivery and to be in a position to catch the baby. Two other women were stationed on either side of the pregnant woman to hold her hands and arms while she was pushing. The midwife and her assistants all participated in the prayers and chants that accompanied this process.

Midwives Provide Spiritual Care

Midwives, along with the pregnant women they were serving, often called on divine help during labor and delivery. The Egyptians believed that help from the gods and goddesses was essential to ensure a healthy child and a safe delivery. Prayers to the goddess Tawaret, for instance, were believed to be especially important. This goddess was often depicted as a pregnant and ferocious-looking hippopotamus, whose very fierceness was believed to keep evil spirits from attacking a woman as she gave birth.

Birthing areas usually contained shrines devoted to the popular dwarf god Bes, who was often depicted dancing and playing instruments in his role as the protector of women in childbirth. Bes's presence was important during deliveries: Through his music and noisy revelry he was supposed to vanquish any evil spirits hovering around the mother and baby. Midwives and their assistants often sang and chanted during difficult deliveries for this reason. In addition, many midwives stamped their feet, shouted, and made loud noises with rattles, drums, and tambourines to drive away evil spirits.

Midwives often incorporated specific magic spells to aid them in the delivery process. Many Egyptian midwives used ivory wands to draw protective circles around the woman giving birth. These wands were also placed on the pregnant woman's abdomen to assist in the driving away of evil spirits. Egyptian historians describe these wands as being "decorated with carvings of the deities, snakes, lions, and crocodiles."[36] The animals, the Egyptians believed, would help keep evil supernatural forces at bay.

This terracotta pitcher depicts a mother breast-feeding her newborn.

Care of the Newborn

Midwives played an important role in the immediate care of the newborn child. After the child was delivered, the midwife tied the umbilical cord with strong thread and severed it, preserving it for a ceremony that introduced the child into an Egyptian community. After delivering the placenta, the part of the uterus that provides protection and food for the fetus, she bathed the child in Nile water and massaged it with various oils and fragrances.

After birth, the midwife thoroughly examined the child to determine its probability of survival. She carefully watched over a sickly newborn, looking for signs of its life expectancy. The Egyptians believed that if the child cried loudly, its chances of survival were good, but if the baby made a sound like the creaking of pine trees or turned its face downward, it would probably die. Where there was doubt, the midwife often advised the mother to feed the infant a diet of milk containing a small fragment of her placenta. If the child did not vomit this mixture, the ancient Egyptians believed it would survive. The midwife further accessed the baby's chances of survival by checking its skin color and facial expression.

Once the midwife assessed the child's condition, she placed healthy children at their mothers' sides. The midwife instructed the mother on how breast–feed and care for the newborn. She also showed new mothers how to bathe the child and how to look for certain symptoms that might suggest an illness. Since different deities were associated with different body parts, the midwife often placed or tied amulets and charms to each part of a child's body to invoke the gods' protection.

Female physicians and midwives were highly sought–after medical practitioners. Many of the women who served in these positions amassed great wealth and were quite respected during their lifetimes. A few, such as Peseshet, the first female physician, were honored as cult figures and were regarded as semidivine. Egyptian women even used statues and small artistic representations of well–known female healers as protection during times of illness. As a group, female medical practitioners served the general public and the elite of Egyptian society alike.

Chapter 5:
Women of the Palace

Living a more luxurious life than anyone else in Egyptian society, the women who lived in the royal palace of ancient Egypt fulfilled many roles. While doing so they enjoyed the finest furnishings and greatest comforts that could be found anywhere in the empire. Members of the royalty lived on sprawling estates with hundreds of servants attending to their every need. Surrounded by riches, royal women, from female pharaohs down to the concubines of the harem, assumed various responsibilities that helped the imperial government run smoothly.

Female Pharaohs

Pharaohs epitomized the very best of Egyptian society and stood at the helm of the government. The position of pharaoh was inherited and was usually passed on to the eldest son of the king's primary wife. However, many noteworthy Egyptian women held the exalted position of pharaoh. Female pharaohs ruled their empire well and had a tremendous impact on Egyptian life and history.

Female pharaohs were the most important women in the palace. It was the pharaoh's duty to uphold order by overcoming Egypt's enemies while also ensuring that her land prospered and grew strong. The everyday lives of female pharaohs were, therefore, filled with affairs of state, receptions, ceremonies, the administration of justice, military campaigns, and other activities related to increasing Egypt's prestige and power.

In 2148 B.C. Neith–Ikret became the first female pharaoh of Egypt. She was long remembered in the Middle East as one of the bravest and most beautiful women of her time. Little, however, is known of her four–year rule. Queen Sebeknefru (1789 to 1786 B.C.) served alongside her young son after the death of Pharoah Amenemhet III, and then ruled as sole pharaoh for several years. She is best remembered for completing many of the building projects that Egypt is known for. Nitocris, Hatshepsut, Nefertiti, and Cleopatra VII also ruled as pharaoh at various points in ancient

Egyptian history and left a lasting mark on Egyptian society.

Female Pharaohs on the Job

Among the many roles and responsibilities of female pharaohs, none was as important as leading the Egyptian army in times of war and conquest. Hatshepsut, who ruled from 1503 to 1482 B.C., for instance, built a great navy for the purpose of trade and warfare. During her reign as pharaoh, the Egyptian navy became a force to be reckoned with and established a vast trading empire. In addition to building a strong navy, Hatshepsut also spent vast sums of money to create a powerful army. On at least one recorded occasion, Hatshepsut personally led her ground troops into battle in order to quell a rebellion in a neighboring region. Egyptian historians explain Hatshepsut's personal involvement: "She had to prove herself a warrior Pharaoh to her people."[37] Most historians agree that by riding into battle with her troops, Hatshepsut showed the Egyptian people that she was willing to fight for them.

In addition to playing a military role, female pharaohs in ancient Egypt were also responsible for sending expeditions to foreign lands. They ordered these missions not only for the purpose of negotiating treaties but also to purchase goods not available in the empire. Several Egyptian expeditionary forces bought and traded for such items as incense, ivory, ebony, and the skins of many exotic animals. Likewise myrrh, frankincense, and other fragrant unguents were obtained in foreign lands to use in Egypt's large cosmetic and perfume industries.

Female pharaohs were also expected to be great patrons of the arts. In this role, they were responsible for the building of great monuments, temples, statues and other architectural masterpieces. These grand structures and artworks in turn reflected positively on the pharoah's reign. Hatshepsut, for instance, ordered the building of two tall, needle–shaped stone monuments, called obelisks, during her reign. Through their very size and magnificence, Hatshepsut proclaimed that she was a great and powerful woman and leader.

Female pharaohs were, in addition to all their other roles, the ceremonial leaders of the Egyptian people. They made frequent public appearances in attempts to solidify their rule and impress the nation with their riches and prestige. They appeared in many spectacular settings for major ritual events and festivals, wearing all the fixings of splendor that signified their status. Donning elaborate headpieces and the finest robes and other clothing, female pharaohs arrived at such ceremonies carried on lavish platforms by servants and slaves.

As the head of vast bureaucracies, female pharaohs employed hundreds of

Queen Hatshepsut, one of Egypt's greatest female pharaohs, makes an offering to the sun god in this carving from her tomb.

advisers. Each pharaoh had numerous counselors, generals, and lawyers to assist them in ruling the country. Ultimately, however, it was the pharaoh who was responsible for administering all the departments of the Egyptian government. These included the distribution of food during times of drought, the control of the labor force, the dispatch of envoys to various countries, and the collection of taxes.

Most female pharaohs were very effective rulers during their years in power in ancient Egypt. Historians agree, for instance, that Hatshepsut was an outstanding pharaoh. The period of her rule was one of the most prosperous in Egyptian history, a time when the people had abundant work, shelter, and food. Her reign was also a time of great peace and advancement in the arts. While other

The obelisk of Queen Hatshepsut stands among the ruins at Karnak as a testament to her importance to Egyptian history.

female rulers both preceded and followed her, Hatshepsut's long and prosperous rule made her one of the greatest female rulers of all time. Historian David Bediz elaborates: "She ruled the most powerful, advanced civilization in the world, successfully for twenty years. . . . Her success stands for all eternity."[38]

The Great Royal Wife

During the reign of male pharaohs, the most important woman in the palace, and in all of Egypt, was the pharaoh's primary wife, called the great royal wife. The great royal wife ranked next to her husband in political and religious significance and is often shown in tomb paintings sitting or standing by the pharaoh's side. Although pharoahs usually had many wives, only one woman held this position at a given time.

Many of the great royal wives were buried in pyramid tombs and were provided with ceremonial boats to sail the heavens with the gods. The magnificence of their funerals attested to their importance in life. They were treasured and worshipped as the epitome of Egyptian beauty. They were expected to set the standard of beauty and behavior for all Egyptian women, and as such, they devoted immense time and expense to positively presenting themselves. For example, the great royal wife Nefertiti was famed throughout the ancient world during the fourteenth century B.C. for her beauty. She served as a role model for all other Egyptian women. Nefertiti's name means "the Beautiful One Has Come," and she was also referred to as "Fair of Face," "Mistress of Joy," "Endowed with Charm," and "Great of Love." Historian Joyce Tyldesley summarizes Nefertiti's appeal: "Standing proud beside her husband, Akhenaten, Nefertiti was the envy of all; a beautiful woman blessed by the sun god, adored by her family, and worshipped by the people. Her image and her name were celebrated throughout the land."[39] Nefertiti and other great royal wives, through their beauty and presence, enhanced the prestige and power of their pharaoh husbands.

The primary political role of the great royal wife was a ceremonial one. For example, Nefertari, the great royal wife of Pharaoh Ramses II, accompanied her husband on several royal processions up the Nile to dedicate various temples built in his honor. Great royal wives also had to be present at all banquets, festivals, and other rituals that their husbands attended. At one temple complex at Abu Simbel, Nefertari was honored above all other queens for her ceremonial role with a colossal statue. Many other great royal wives were remembered by their husbands in a similar fashion, with statues, paintings, and other artistic representations depicting the women who accompanied the pharaoh on ceremonial occasions.

Queen Nefertiti (left) was adored by her subjects as a paragon of beauty.

Like the pharaoh, a great royal wife was believed to be semidivine; as such, she was given all the honors befitting a goddess. These women were believed to have the special blessing of both Isis, the mythical goddess queen of Egypt, and also Hathor, the goddess of women. Great royal wives, in fact, wore crowns that linked them to these two goddesses. During religious ceremonies, many great royal wives acted out the role of Isis and Hathor. In these roles, they officiated at the many Egyptian temples dedicated to the goddesses, leading prayers and making offerings during temple ceremonies.

Great royal wives did not necessarily play an active role in political life. They held no political position per se, and they did not speak out publicly about political issues. Their influence, instead, was more covert, with many wives becoming the power behind the throne. Great Royal Wife Tiy, for instance, was an astute woman of great ability who became a powerful and influential figure during the reign of her husband, Amenhotep III. Tiy corresponded with dozens of Middle Eastern leaders through letters and other documents that have survived. Journalist Rumoko Rashidi describes the significance of these letters: "She was such an integral part of [Egyptian political] affairs that on more than one occasion, foreign sovereigns appealed to her directly in matters of international significance."[40] Tiy continued her correspondence following the death of her husband and used her political knowledge and diplomatic ties to help her son Akhenaton, the new pharaoh, increase his power.

The Queen Mother

After the great royal wife, the queen mother, or mother of the pharaoh, was the next most important woman in the palace. The ancient Egyptians believed that the queen mother was especially close to the gods and was considered divine because she had produced a son who became pharaoh.

Indeed, queen mothers were viewed as the epitome of motherhood in ancient Egypt. In a symbolic way, by giving birth to the rulers of Egypt, queen mothers were regarded as the mothers of Egypt. Numerous tomb paintings and other art forms have given modern scholars an inside look at the importance of such women in ancient Egyptian society.

Many tomb paintings show the pharaoh's mother standing next to him or slightly behind him. As mother of the ruling monarch, queen mothers in Egypt often played a significant role in influencing their sons' decisions regarding matters of state and other important issues.

Queen Tiy, perhaps the best–known queen mother, gained prominence not

Queen Tiy (right) gained prominence as both the great royal wife of Pharaoh Amenhotep (left) and the mother of Pharaoh Akhenaton.

only as the great royal wife of Amenhotep III but also as the mother of Pharaoh Akhenaton. Historian Tyldesley summarizes her importance: "Tiy was effectively the power behind two thrones, not only ruling on behalf of her . . . husband, but exerting a strong . . . influence over her young son."[41]

The King's Wife

In addition to the great royal wife, Egyptian pharaohs were often married to many other women who held the simple title of king's wife or royal wife. Some of these women were chosen from among the elite classes, some were members of his royal family, and still others were the daughters of rulers from neighboring countries. The wife's status and role in the royal family varied a great deal; whereas some had considerable power and played important roles, others had little political influence. These wives, along with their servants, spent most of their time in the women's quarters, called *ipet*, located close to the palace. It was in these quarters that the king's wives brought up their children—the sons and daughters of the pharaoh.

King's wives became especially important when the great royal wife was unable to produce a male heir. In these situations, minor royal wives could increase their power in the palace if they were able to influence the royal line of succession by giving birth to sons. Producing a male heir gave many of these wives additional power and prestige. In several cases, such women were elevated to a position just slightly less important than that of the great royal wife. In a few instances, a king's wife might even take her place alongside the pharaoh and fill the role of his great royal wife, along with the incumbent responsibilities.

Royal Daughters

Although sons were very valuable, the daughters of the pharaoh were also important members of the royal palace. As the children of royalty, the girls prepared early for the many duties they would have in Egyptian royal society. These included attending and participating in ritual ceremonies as part of the royal family, being available to marry other members of royalty, and preparing themselves for becoming queen.

At puberty, the pharaoh's daughters began the specialized training that was required for a person who might someday become queen. The education of royal daughters stressed morality and good manners, but most girls also studied the fundamentals of reading, writing, and mathematics. A few daughters, such as Hatshepsut, grew up under their father's personal tutelage and were educated in much the same way young princes were. Cleopatra VII was another

This painting depicts royal siblings enjoying leisure time with their cats. From an early age, the daughters of royalty were groomed as queens.

well–educated daughter. She studied with tutors and became proficient in six different languages, an unusual accomplishment for any person in ancient Egypt. She was also knowledgeable in mathematics, philosophy, art, music, and medicine—talents she would use later when she became pharaoh.

Royal daughters were expected to attend many of the same ceremonies and festivities that their parents did. Female children were expected to serve as role models for all Egyptian children, just as their parents served in similar fashion for adults. As such, the pharaoh's daughters were viewed by the public as examples of what was expected of children: to be well behaved, obedient, and perfectly dressed and groomed.

With the knowledge that they would one day be queen, royal daughters were also expected to be available for marriage to their fathers, brothers, or a son of a secondary wife in order to keep the throne and the title in the family. The editors of Time–Life Books explain: "The practice of [royal] men marrying their daughters and sisters had deep roots in Egyptian culture and theology."[42] This practice, the Egyptians believed, kept the ruling line pure. When the great royal wife, for instance, was unable to produce a male heir, her oldest daughter was often required to marry a son from one of the pharaoh's secondary wives. This kind of marriage, the Egyptians believed, legitimized the reign of the new pharaoh. The ancient Egyptians also believed that interfamilial marriages served to strengthen the family's power and prestige. The Egyptians justified this practice because many of their gods and goddesses had married in this fashion.

Queens as Coregent

Upon a pharoah's death, many great royal wives and a few king's wives served as co–regents, or corulers, for their young sons until they were ready to assume command of the Egyptian government. In her role as coregent, an Egyptian queen assumed the full roles and responsibilities of the pharaoh. As her son neared maturity, the queen usually ruled side by side with him, teaching him what he would need to become pharaoh. When the boy reached maturity, the queen usually stepped aside but continued to advise him from the background.

A few royal daughters also became coregents and ruled with their fathers in such a manner. Shortly after the death of her mother, for instance, Hatshepsut took the Egyptian throne alongside her pharaoh father. Many historians believe that she had equal responsibilities and duties as that of her father. Hatshepsut's name was depicted together with her father's name in royal writings and tomb art of the period.

Sometimes, royal daughters served as corulers with their younger brothers. In these cases, the daughters often married their brothers and ruled as pharaohs until the young men were old enough to take over the leadership of the empire. Following the death of her father, Hatshepsut, for instance, served as coregent for her young half brother and new husband, Thutmose II. For the most part, Hatshepsut had full control of state affairs and used this time to gather power and influence among her father's advisers, playing a dominant role in the Egyptian government. She would later take the throne herself, becoming pharaoh.

Cleopatra VII began her rule in much the same manner. She served as coregent for her younger brother, the ten–year–old Ptolemy XIII. Cleopatra, a capable young woman, held the reins of government for a number of years. By the time Ptolemy XIII was old enough to rule Egypt, Cleopatra had elicited Roman support

Cleopatra VII

Cleopatra VII, the last pharaoh of Egypt, was born in 69 B.C. The daughter of Ptolemy XII, Cleopatra grew to be a charming and clever young woman. She had a keen intellect and was a woman of powerful ambition. She wanted to be the ruler of ancient Egypt and took a number of ruthless steps to ensure that she would become pharaoh.

After the deaths of her brothers at her instigation, Cleopatra aligned herself and her nation with the powerful Roman Empire. She made diplomatic alliances with ruler Julius Caesar and later his successor, Mark Antony. These ties would ultimately prove to be her downfall. To provide a massive army to assist Antony, Cleopatra moved Egypt into debt. Food shortages, unemployment, and drought marked her years in power. In addition, her romantic liaisons with Caesar and Antony left Egypt open to foreign conquest and ultimately led to the end of the ancient Egyptian empire.

Cleopatra VII commands her fleet in battle against the enemies of Roman lover Mark Antony.

and ousted her brother, taking over the role of pharaoh herself.

Servants, Slaves, and Other Royal Assistants

Women of royalty were not the only women in the palace. Hundreds of female servants and slaves lived and worked there. Each member of the royal family, their advisers, and government bureaucrats required a large retinue of servants and slaves to assist them in their daily living. A dozen or more women, for instance, helped each royal daughter bathe and dress for the day, and the great royal wife might employ several dozen female servants to perform a wide variety of duties. These duties included helping the pharaoh's wife with personal hygiene, cleaning the royal quarters, teaching the royal children, and accompanying the royal women to all festivities and ceremonies.

One of the most important positions held by these women was that of the royal wet nurse. While not members of the royal family, they were called "royal" because of their importance to the pharaoh's family. Wet nurses were carefully chosen from the ranks of the wives of high-ranking court officials. While wealthy women often used a servant for this position, the women of the palace relied on a woman of wealth and title. The royal wet nurse was responsible for providing her own breast milk to a royal infant. The feeding of a royal child was so important that it could not be entrusted to a mere servant or slave. Thus, the royal wet nurse was a valued member of the royal family and was given the responsibility of being in charge of those servants attending the children. Historian Tyldesley explains the importance of this position: "The role of wet nurse to the royal family was one of the most important and influential positions that a non-royal woman could achieve, conferring great honor—and great privileges upon her own baby . . . who was raised [and educated] alongside the royal child."[43]

An Egyptian prince shares a moment of tenderness with a royal servant.

The Harem

Hundreds of other Egyptian women served as concubines in the pharaoh's harem. Large harems were common in ancient Egypt and date back to the ear-

Intrigue Among the Women in the Palace

Kings' wives and the women of the harem often became involved in plots to influence the pharaoh to pick their sons as the heir to the throne. In his book *Ancient Egypt*, historian David Silverman recounts one such plot: "A document from the reign of Ramsesses III relates to a failed conspiracy hatched . . . by a royal wife . . . who plotted to kill Ramsesses and put her son on the throne." A group of priests, courtiers, and ladies of the harem joined the royal wife in this particular plot. Using a book of destructive magic from the royal library, the conspirators made potions to paralyze the guards, along with written spells and wax figures with which to harm the pharaoh. The plot ultimately failed, and the conspirators, including the royal wife and her son, were tried for sorcery and condemned to death.

Female pharaohs were also involved in plots to enhance their power. Nitocris, for instance, decided to take revenge after her husband Pepi II was assassinated in 2180 B.C. After assuming the throne, Nitocris invited her husband's assassins to attend a dinner at the palace, a sprawling estate on the banks of the Nile. From what historians can determine, once the guests began their meal, Nitocris opened the gates connecting the Nile channel to the large dining room, drowning her enemies.

liest periods of Egyptian history. The women of the harem came from various backgrounds and were responsible for giving the pharaoh pleasure and companionship. They were also responsible for providing him with many children. For the most part, their names were not recorded and their children were largely ignored in royal histories of the time. One of the largest harems reported by Egyptian historians is that of Amenhotep III. His harem was enormous, containing more than one thousand women.

The hundreds of women of the harem had to be available to the pharaoh at any time of the day or night. At all times, therefore, they had to keep themselves bathed and finely dressed so that they would be pleasing and attractive to the pharaoh when he called on them. These women came from all walks and classes of Egyptian society. Women of foreign and noble birth made up the majority of the harem, with an occasional peasant woman also earning a place. These women and their children possessed no legal claim on the pharaoh, except in a few cases where a member of the harem was elevated to the position of king's wife because she had borne the pharaoh a son.

In addition to providing a home for the pharaoh's concubines, the harem was also a center of industry, education, and even agriculture. Full–time resident administrators supervised a staff of specialized female artisans and servants. Hundreds of young Egyptian women, for instance, were trained in the harem's textile workshops in the craft of spinning and weaving fine linen cloth. These women furnished clothing for the pharaoh and his family. Others wove baskets and similar items.

In addition to the textile workshops, most harems maintained their own farms, raising wheat and barley along with livestock of various kinds. Many women of the harem worked in the fields, sowing seeds and then helping with the harvest. These women were instrumental in providing the palace with all the grain they would need for the year. Women also tended the palace livestock, which included cows, goats, chickens, sheep, and other animals. The ladies of the harem sheered sheep, made wool and leather clothing from the skins, and made sure the animals were fed and watered. Still other harem women worked in small vegetable gardens. Each woman of the harem was expected to keep herself busy during the day by working in some capacity.

Whether fulfilling ceremonial, military, political, or practical responsibilities, the women of the palace ensured a well–run government and royal house. Many of their names have been lost to history, but from the records that have survived, historians and scholars have been able to learn much about the women of the palace and their roles in ancient Egyptian society.

Chapter 6: Professional Women of Ancient Egypt

Women in ancient Egypt functioned as equals with men in business, law, government, and other professional fields. Few positions in Egyptian society were closed to them. Thus, professional women in ancient Egypt held a variety of important positions within the community and the empire. They served as professional dancers, managers, overseers, lawyers, soldiers, and scribes, and a few held high positions within the pharaoh's government. Well paid and highly respected, professional women were valuable members of Egyptian society and made many important contributions to the power and prestige of the Egyptian empire.

Professional Dancers

Dancing was an important part of life in ancient Egypt and had its origins in religious ritual. Egyptian women from all walks of life were hired to perform as dancers at various festivities and ceremonies. These women danced during temple rites, festivals, and funerals, and they often impersonated goddesses as part of their routine. Dancers typically wore special costumes and masks to make themselves appear like a goddess and followed specific patterns of steps that imitated the deity's characteristics and attributes.

Professional dancers were in great demand at the lavish parties given by the wealthy and the royal family. Anywhere from a dozen to a hundred female dancers might be hired to entertain the guests at these festivities. Many high–ranking households, in fact, maintained their own private troupe of dancers. In well–rehearsed routines, the dancers spun, flowed, and encircled the banquet hall. Historians Bob Brier and Hoyt Hobbs describe the women's performance: "They are often depicted bending backward in gymnastic–like contortions as their long hair, tied at the ends with weights that swayed to the music, touched the ground."[44]

Professional dancers were also hired to perform at the coronations of Egyptian pharaohs. Dressed in elaborate and expensive outfits, these female dancers accompanied the pharaohs as they were

Professional dancers like these were popular performers at parties given by wealthy Egyptian families.

carried on platforms to their coronation ceremony. Cleopatra VII was particularly known for her use of female dancers. When she first met her future lover Mark Antony of Rome, she arrived at his ship accompanied by her servants and dozens of dancers dressed like mermaids and goddesses. During the lavish banquet that followed, the dancers performed for the pharaoh and her guest.

Any female whose beauty or skill caught the attention of a rich or royal person might be asked to serve as a professional dancer. Female dancers were very acrobatic and could perform back bends, headstands, and cartwheels. They usually performed naked or with a brief sash around the waist. These talented women were in great demand throughout ancient Egypt.

Most female dancers learned their skills either from relatives or in professional dance schools. They were then hired on as apprentices to a dance troupe. Most dance troupes were run by other professional women, who arranged for bookings throughout the empire.

Female dancers were greatly respected in ancient Egypt and were immortalized in tomb art and statues. They were also well rewarded for their talents, receiving riches and other appreciative tokens of their skills.

Perfume Makers

Another profession dominated by Egyptian women was perfume making. Women in ancient Egypt made perfume by wringing out a bag crammed with flower petals in such a way that they released a precious essence. This liquid was then used to scent a large jar of oil. Professional perfume manufacturers added ingredients such as cinnamon and myrrh to this mixture to create a variety of different aromas.

Female perfume manufacturers used several other techniques for extracting the scents from flowers, seeds, and fruits to make their perfumes. One was enfleurage, a technique during which the women pressed plant material into trays of animal

Perfume makers press lilies as they prepare an extract. The profession of perfume making in ancient Egypt was dominated by women.

fat. They heated the fat in an oven or left it out in the sun to warm. The melted fat was strained and left to cool and harden. In this way, the women made solid scented unguents that could be used as fragrances for the skin and hair.

Women perfume makers made use of yet another technique, called steam distillation, to make perfume. In this process, the women subjected various plants to steam produced by a burning fire. The heat caused the plant to release scented oils that were skimmed off the surface of the water and were then used in perfumes.

One of the most popular scents that female perfume makers knew how to produce was known as oil of lilies. To make this perfume, the women used a thousand Madonna lilies that they grew in special gardens.

Linen Producers

Ancient Egyptian women also played an important role in linen production. Women held a full range of jobs within the linen production field, ranging from weavers to supervisors. Female supervisors were hired by the wealthy and royalty to oversee hundreds of other Egyptian women working on large estates and at the palace in the production of fine linen.

These professional linen producers worked in big weaving rooms with each group of women responsible for one particular task. Once that task was complete, the items were passed to the next group in a manner similar to modern assembly lines. Their jobs were generally very hard and their hours long.

Female linen producers primarily worked with flax, a slender plant cultivated for its fibers. During the first stage of linen production, the female workers would "ret" the flax. This involved soaking it to remove the outer casing of each stalk. The long linen fibers found inside were then softened. Next, the women joined, twisted, and spun the fibers using a simple spindle. Historians Brier and Hobbs describe this process:

> Egyptian spindles consisted of a wooden shaft, four inches or more in length, through which a whorl—a two to four inch disk—was attached. . . . The fiber was tied to a groove at the top of the shaft, then the spindle was rolled vigorously down the spinner's thigh which set it spinning, stretching the fiber. . . . while twisting it for strength.[45]

This process produced thread, which the women wound into hanks or balls. After producing the thread, Egyptian women used looms to make cloth.

Ancient Egyptian women were using looms as far back as 3000 B.C. They originally used a horizontal loom that was

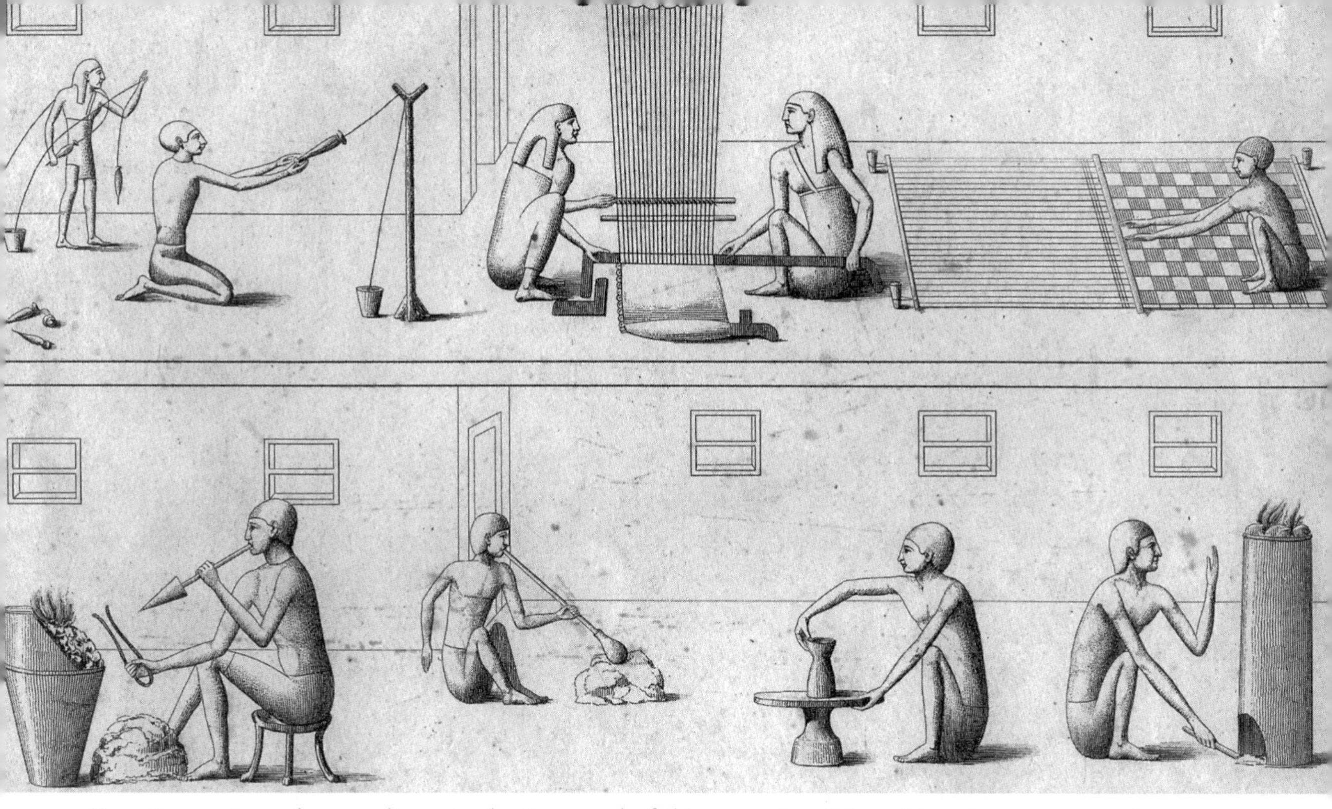

Egyptians spin and weave linen in the top panel of this engraving. Many Egyptian women made a living by producing fine linen.

made up of two wooden beams anchored to the floor by short pegs. Working this kind of loom required the women to kneel, bend over, or sit on the floor. The work was backbreaking, long, and somewhat tedious, but the women were compensated for their work with payments of food, clothing, and other goods.

Women in Politics

A few women of ancient Egypt held government positions. One of the most exalted of these titles in ancient Egypt was that of vizier, or prime minister. Vizier was the highest political rank below that of the pharaoh; only a few women attained this important position. According to ancient documents, a royal woman named Nebet held this title during the Sixth Dynasty and was officially called "Vizier, Judge, and Magistrate." As vizier, she was responsible for receiving foreign dignitaries, negotiating treaties, and overseeing judicial decisions and the making of laws. She was also expected to oversee the high court, where the most serious crimes in Egypt were tried.

Hundreds of women served in politics through a variety of other government positions. Women served on legal committees and helped formulate laws. Others accompanied the pharaoh on diplomatic missions, acting as advisers in matters of foreign policy and Egyptian expansion into other lands. Women often accompanied their husbands as special envoys to foreign lands. These women proved adept at negotiating treaties and at arranging for the marriage of foreign princesses to the pharaoh. Other women served as the pharaoh's special traders. They were responsible for acquiring exotic foods and products from foreign lands and for making these items available for the pharaoh's use. The women who served in these roles were well trained and respected within the royal community.

Female Scribes

A number of ancient Egyptian women held the important position of scribe. Scribes were essential to running the Egyptian government. Female scribes did everything from copying religious texts and filing diplomatic letters to collecting taxes, paying workers, recording court cases, and organizing building projects and trading expeditions. In addition to their writing skills, these professional women were valued because of their knowledge of mathematics and their ability to calculate long sums.

Female scribes generally learned the skills of reading, writing, and mathematics from their fathers and brothers. A few scribes attended the same training schools that their male counterparts did. To do their jobs, scribes used an oblong palette with two round holes for cakes of red and black ink. This palette had a long groove in it that held reed pens that scribes used for writing. A scribe also used a small pot of water to wet her ink, a knife for trimming the sheets of papyrus reed, and a stone for smoothing the paper's surface.

One job of female scribes was to translate and interpret ancient texts to be used by the masses. The ancient Egyptians produced a massive amount of literature, including detailed medical texts, philosophical works, poems, and law reports. It was the responsibility of female scribes to be familiar with three different kinds of ancient writing: hieroglyphics, Greek, and an early Egyptian script called demotic. Female scribes were able to translate these languages into an everyday Egyptian script, understandable to all. Some texts were so lengthy that many female scribes spent their entire lifetimes working on them.

A few women worked as scribes for the priests and priestesses of Egypt, recording information about sick people who were healed in the temple. These women also documented the various landholdings and property that belonged to the temple. Most of the female scribes who worked at the temples were proficient in all known forms of mathematics. It was necessary for them to record the value of land and other property, and

Female Scribes and Hieroglyphics

Egyptian hieroglyphics date back to the beginning of the ancient Egyptian empire. The word itself is taken from the Greek language and means "sacred carving." Each hieroglyphic picture stood for an object or a sound. Hieroglyphics were carved on papyrus, a tall reed nearly thirteen feet high that grew throughout the marshes of Egypt. To make papyrus rolls, the pith of the plant was taken out of the reeds and then cut into strips that were pounded until a thin product was produced. This material was then polished and put into a long roll.

The Egyptians left thousands of papyrus documents for future historians to examine. Women scribes undoubtedly wrote many of these scrolls. It was not until 1822 that scholars were able to decipher what the hieroglyphics meant. In 1799 French general and leader Napoléon Bonaparte led an army into Egypt, where they discovered what is now referred to as the Rosetta Stone. French historians found three different languages written on this stone: hieroglyphics, an earlier Egyptian script called demotic, and Greek. Using the Greek language as a guide, scholars cracked the code in 1822, allowing historians to finally read the writing of ancient Egypt. As a result of this remarkable achievement, modern historians have been able to learn a great deal about life in ancient Egypt.

Many of the scribes who carved the hieroglyphics on papyrus scrolls such as this one were women.

they also had to calculate the profits from the sale of produce and other products.

Another task that sometimes fell to women scribes was that of the "sealer." These were women who fastened the pharaoh's treasury or food storerooms' doors with seals to keep the valuable contents safe. No keys or locks were available in ancient Egypt, so doors were usually sealed with small lumps of mud. Once properly closed, the door could only be opened by breaking the seal.

Women in Law

One of the most important professions open to women was that of the law. A number of ancient Egyptian women studied the law and served as lawyers and judges in the Egyptian courts. No law schools operated in ancient Egypt, but the women who aspired to a legal career often studied and apprenticed themselves to established lawyers. During their time in training, they read legal documents, attended trials of all kinds, and often assisted their teachers in preparing and presenting cases in the courts.

Female lawyers worked in two types of courts: the local courts, or *kenbet*, and the high court. Local courts dealt with all legal cases except those that involved capital punishment or execution. The latter cases were tried in the high court, usually located in the pharaoh's palace and presided over by the vizier. Female lawyers were responsible for presenting all kinds of evidence at both courts. The verdict was announced by the presiding judge after a thorough examination of the evidence.

Ancient Egyptian women had the right to bring lawsuits against anyone in

Female Musicians

Female musicians were widely employed in ancient Egypt to entertain nobles in their homes. Tomb scenes show the wealthy listening to performances by female singers and female musicians. These women also performed at burial ceremonies, reciting special songs that either urged the living to enjoy life to the fullest or emphasized the joys of the afterlife.

Many women also played in small orchestras. The most common instrument they used was the lute, which was similar to a guitar. The lute's strings were plucked with a pick called a plectrum, while the instrument's long neck was attached to a tortoise–shell soundbox. Women also played flutes, clarinets, and pipes made of wood. To lay down the rhythm, they used drums, tambourines, ivory or wooden clappers, and large bead collars that could be shaken or rattled. Other common instruments used by women included a finger drum called a *darra boukah*; an oboe, called a *nay*; and a little violin called a *rebaba*.

Egyptian women loved to sing, and the festivals offered them a time to perform with others. Women sang love songs and songs that honored the gods. Some women sang in choirs, and others were hired by the wealthy to perform at banquets and ceremonies. Singing was also used in the treatment of the sick.

open court and there was, according to Egyptian historians, "no gender–based bias against them [for there were] many cases of women winning their claims."[46] Many legal documents have been discovered by modern archaeologists that attest to Egyptian women bringing their cases before the court. Female lawyers were often hired to present these cases. Female lawyers also took on the cases of male Egyptians and presented their cases to courts throughout the land. In several instances, the local magistrates or judges who heard the cases and ruled on a verdict were also female.

In a few recorded cases, both the plaintiff and the defendant were female. In one such case, a woman named Irynofret, the wife of a civil servant, had purchased a young Syrian slave girl from a traveling merchant. She paid for this slave using bartered goods such as linen dresses, household wares, and other items. Shortly after the deal was closed, a woman named Bakmut lodged an official complaint that she, not Irynofret, was the girl's owner and demanded a share of the slave's services. The two women appeared before a magistrate and pleaded their cases by presenting evidence and testimony. The presiding magistrate, according to an ancient papyrus, directed Irynofret to make a formal declaration of her innocence. "Swear an oath by the Sovereign," he ordered, "saying thus: 'If witnesses establish against me that any property of the lady Bakmut was included in my payment for this slave–girl, and I have concealed it, then I shall be liable for 100 strokes, having also forfeited her.'"[47] Irynofret apparently complied with the request and swore her oath. Witnesses for both sides were called to the stand. The verdict of the magistrate has, unfortunately, been lost to history and the outcome of the case remains unknown.

Hundreds of Egyptian women appeared in front of the court in quite a different role. These were the women accused of various crimes against others and the state. Women were charged with a variety of crimes, including theft, nonpayment of debt, selling property they did not own, not caring for their sick relatives, and murder. Women were allowed to have a lawyer defend them, but often there was little the attorney could do. A woman named Nesmut, for example, was implicated in a series of robberies of the royal tombs in the Valley of the Kings during the Twentieth Dynasty and was punished for her crimes.

Punishments for female defendants were severe and were intended to deter future offenses. Minor misdemeanors were often punished with one hundred strokes of a whip, confinement in a local prison, or a sentence of forced labor in Egyptian fields or textile workshops.

Women who were found guilty of adultery might suffer the amputation of a body part or be burned to death. Temporary leniency was granted to a pregnant woman, at least until her child was born. Following the delivery of the child, the woman was usually executed.

Female lawyers and defendants often prayed and worshipped Ma'at, the goddess of truth. The entire ancient Egyptian legal system, in fact, was governed by a concept known as *ma'at*, meaning order or right, as personified by the goddess of the same name. Historian David Silverman explains this concept as it applied to law: "For the Egyptians themselves, the ma'at was both social justice and moral right-

Ma'at, the goddess of truth, embraces an Egyptian queen in her winged arms. Female lawyers and defendants prayed to Ma'at to help ensure a fair trial.

eousness; the need for the powerful not to exploit the weak, and for all people to live in harmony."[48] Female lawyers prayed to the goddess to ensure that their legal dealings were always honorable and served the truth, and female defendants appealed to Ma'at for leniency and fair treatment.

Military Women

Hundreds of women served in the ancient Egyptian army as camp helpers, soldiers, and, occasionally, as military commanders. These women proved indispensable on a number of occasions in Egyptian history, often making the difference between defeat and victory. Historian Joann Fletcher summarizes the military role played by Egyptian women: "The potential for female aggression is reflected in texts and in depictions of women stabbing soldiers, firing arrows, and physically overpowering men—images supported by the weapons found with female burials."[49]

Many Egyptian women followed their husbands into battle and served as camp followers, marching with the army into hostile lands. These women provided meals, comfort, and medical care to the male soldiers. Behind the battle lines, these women tended the wounds of soldiers, and sometimes performed minor surgeries to remove arrows and spear points. Sometimes, the camp helpers saw battle action themselves: They often took their husbands' places on the front lines when the men were wounded or killed.

A number of royal women played significant military roles during the reigns of their husbands. For instance, Queen Tetisheri, the wife of Pharaoh Sekenenre, founded a long line of victorious warrior queens. She was active when Egypt was seriously threatened by invading Hyksos warriors from Palestine during the second millennium B.C. Thanks to the efforts of these warrior queens, the Hyksos were turned back, enabling Egypt to consolidate its power. Historian David E. Jones explains: "The ultimate liberation from this invasion came between 1580 B.C. and 1510 B.C. and was engineered largely by three Egyptian queens: a mother, daughter, and granddaughter."[50]

Queen Tetisheri helped her husband develop battle plans and then helped execute them from her headquarters in Luxor. Tetisheri's daughter, Ahotep, later rallied a large contingent of retreating Egyptian troops after her husband was killed in battle. Ahotep's surviving son, Ahmose, reports on his mother's efforts: "She cared for the soldiers, she brought back her fugitives, gathered up her deserters; she has pacified the south and expelled [the] rebels."[51] In her rich burial tomb, Ahotep was surrounded by the weapons she used along with several golden military decorations she had been awarded, including the Order of the Fly, ancient Egypt's highest military decoration. Ahotep's daughter, Queen Thothmes, continued the fight until the Hyksos were driven out of Egypt for good.

A number of other ancient Egyptian women served in the military. Arsinoë II Philadelphus, the daughter of Pharaoh Ptolemy I, for instance, had a well–deserved reputation as a soldier. In 275 B.C. she joined the military campaign of her brother, who was waging war in Syria. After watching him lose battle after battle, Arsinoë took command of the troops; with her planning and battlefield leadership, she reversed his losses and defeated the Syrians. Archaeologists have found numerous depictions of Egyptian women leading troops into battle and fighting alongside their fathers, husbands, and brothers.

A cameo depicts Ptolemy I and his daughter Arsinoe, who served in the Egyptian military.

Other Professional Women

Another, much less dangerous, profession for ancient Egyptian women was estate management. Wealthy noblemen or members of the royal classes who were either widowed or divorced often hired professional women to oversee their homes and property. Working in luxurious homes and palaces, these women supervised servants, ordered food supplies, planned parties, and kept accurate records of crops and produce. One such woman was described in surviving documents as "the Keeper of the Dining Hall." This woman was in charge of all domestic aspects of a wealthy man's estate and life.

Thousands of Egyptian women, in fact, sought employment outside the house. Peasant women did so to help feed and clothe their families, whereas wealthy women with time on their hands occasionally took jobs out of boredom or because of a desire to cultivate an interest or skill. Many women operated small businesses out of their homes, selling baskets, clothing, vegetables, and other items to the community. Others held positions of great trust and respect and served as treasurers or supervisors in small businesses within their village.

There is documented proof that Egyptian women held other professional positions as well. One ancient manuscript, for instance, describes a number of women who worked as professional florists. These women owned small shops in Egyptian neighborhoods. They catered to the wealthy, who typically ordered flowers, decorative plants, and other items for their homes. Female florists were experts on the types of flowers that could be grown in different soils and what flowers and decorative plants belonged together in gardens. These women could arrange beautiful bouquets and elaborate headpieces made of flowers. Many female florists earned respectable livings and were in great demand in their communities.

Egyptian florists string garlands of roses. Female florists were among the many professional women who earned a living in ancient Egypt.

Another professional position held by Egyptian women was that of beautician. These women worked in a fashion similar to modern–day beauticians. They were well versed in the most popular hairstyles of the time and were well known for the elaborate wigs they made for the wealthy and nobility. Most female beauticians were hired to work in the homes of the elite, but a few owned small shops or operated businesses out of their homes. These women were also adept at applying cosmetics such as eye shadow and were employed by Egyptian men and women who were preparing themselves for important events.

Yet another professional position held by women was that of pilot. Indeed, a few Egyptian women piloted the various boats that sailed up and down the Nile. Most of these women learned about boats and navigation from their fathers and brothers. A few owned their own boats and made a decent profit ferrying produce, livestock, and people to destinations along the river. Professional female pilots were widely respected in ancient Egypt for their skills and knowledge of the ancient waterways.

The professional women of ancient Egypt functioned in a variety of roles during the three–thousand–year history of that civilization. With equal rights and responsibilities, women were respected and admired not only for their beauty and appearance but also for their professional skills and talents. Nowhere else in the ancient world did women hold the number of jobs that Egyptian women did.

Notes

Introduction: "She Was in Every Respect His Equal"

1. Brian M. Fagan. *World Prehistory.* Upper Saddle River, NJ: Prentice Hall, 2003, p. 233.
2. Crystalinks, "Women in Ancient Egypt," www.crystalinks.com/egyptianwomen.html.
3. Rumoko Rashidi, "The African Woman as Heroine," *Michigan Citizen*, September 28, 2002.
4. James Henry Breasted, *A History of Egypt.* Safety Harbor, FL: Simon, 2001, p. 85.

Chapter One: The Peasant Woman

5. Bob Edwards, "Egypt's Golden Empire," *Morning Edition*, National Public Radio, February 27, 2002.
6. Bob Brier and Hoyt Hobbs, *Daily Life of the Ancient Egyptians*, Westport, CT: Greenwood, 1999, p. 107.
7. Rosalie David, *Handbook of Life in Ancient Egypt.* New York: Facts On File, 1998, p 290.
8. Pharaonic Egypt, "Ancient Egyptian Basketry," http://nefertiti.iwebland.com/basketry/index.html.
9. Holly Laite, "Differences in Gender," EMuseum, Minnesota State University, Mankato, www.mnsu.edu/emuseum/prehistory/dailylife/genders/htm.
10. Egypt State Information Service, "Stockbreeding and the Hunt," www.sis.gov.eg/pharo–html/huntfrm.htm.

Chapter Two: A Life of Luxury and Leisure

11. David Silverman, *Ancient Egypt*, New York: Oxford University Press, 1997, p. 83.
12. Editors of Time–Life Books, *Ramses II: Magnificence on the Nile.* Alexandria, VA: Time–Life, 1993, p. 99.
13. Joann Fletcher, *Ancient Egypt: Life, Myth, and Art.* New York: Barnes and Noble, 1999, p. 36.
14. Breasted, *A History of Egypt*, p. 89.
15. Kozue Takahashi, "Ancient Egyptian Hairstyles," EMuseum, Minnesota State University, Mankato, www.mnsu.edu/emuseum/prehistory/egypt/dailylife/hairstyles.html.

16. Zahi Hawass, "Egypt's Hidden Tombs Revealed," *National Geographic*, September 2001, p. 40.
17. Breasted, *A History of Egypt*, p. 90.
18. Silverman, *Ancient Egypt*, p. 165.

Chapter Three: Women and Religion

19. Brier and Hobbs, *Daily Life of the Ancient Egyptians*, p. 33.
20. David, *Handbook of Life in Ancient Egypt*, p. 114.
21. Betina Knapp, "The Archetypal Woman Fulfilled: Isis," *Symposium*, March 1, 1996.
22. Fletcher, *Ancient Egypt*, p. 66.
23. Silverman, *Ancient Egypt*, p. 86.
24. Kent R. Weeks, "Valley of the Kings," *National Geographic*, September 1998, p. 19.
25. Quoted in Fletcher, *Ancient Egypt*, p. 124.
26. Silverman, *Ancient Egypt*, p. 87.
27. Editors of Time–Life Books, *What Life Was Like on the Bank of the Nile.* Alexandria, VA: Time–Life, 1997, p. 55.

Chapter Four: Women in Medicine

28. Quoted in Ahmes L. Pahor, "Medicine and Surgery in Ancient Egypt," Centre for the History of Medicine, http://medweb.bham.ac.uk/histmed/pahor.html.
29. Quoted in Ancient Egypt: Medicine, "Ancient Egyptian Medicine" www.reshafim.org.il/ad/egypt/timelines/topics/medicine.htm.
30. Quoted in Sameh M. Arab, "Medicine in Ancient Egypt," Arab World Books, www.arabworldbooks.com/articles8.htm.
31. Silverman, *Ancient Egypt*, p. 84.
32. Quoted in "Ancient Egyptian Medicine."
33. Quoted in Arab, "Medicine in Ancient Egypt."
34. Silverman, *Ancient Egypt*, p. 84.
35. Quoted in Petra Habiger, "Early History: Menstruation, Menstrual Hygiene, and Woman's Health in Ancient Egypt," Museum of Menstruation and Woman's Health, www.mum.org/ germnt5.htm.
36. Alison Thiele, "Ancient Egyptian Midwifery and Childbirth," EMusuem, Minnesota State University, Mankato, 2002. www.mnsu.edu/emuseum/prehistory/egypt/dailylife/midwifery.htm.

Chapter Five: Women of the Palace

37. Caroline Seawright, "Hatshepsut, Female Pharaoh of Egypt," Tour Egypt, www.touregypt.net/historicalessays/hatshepsut.htm.
38. David Bediz, "The Story of Hatshepsut," Portraits by Bulent Bediz, www.bediz.com/hatshep/story.html.

39. Joyce Tyldesley, *Nefertiti: Egypt's Sun Queen.* New York: Viking, 1998, p. 1.
40. Rashidi, "The African Woman as Heroine."
41. Tyldesley, *Nefertiti*, p. 5.
42. Editors of Time–Life Books, *Ramses II*, p. 88.
43. Tyldesley, *Nefertiti*, p. 47.

Chapter Six: Professional Women of Ancient Egypt

44. Brier and Hobbs, *Daily Life of the Ancient Egyptians*, p. 92.
45. Brier and Hobbs, *Daily Life of the Ancient Egyptians*, p. 118.
46. *Crystalinks*, "Women in Ancient Egypt."
47. Quoted in Editors of Time–Life Books, *Ramses II*, p. 99.
48. Silverman, *Ancient Egypt*, p. 139.
49. Fletcher, *Ancient Egypt*, p. 35.
50. David E. Jones, *Women Warriors.* Washington, DC: Brassey's, 1997, p. 106.
51. Quoted in Fletcher, *Ancient Egypt*, p. 94.

For Further Reading

Books

Joanna Defrates, *What Do We Know About the Egyptians?* New York: Peter Bedrick, 1991. The author focuses on the early Egyptians and their way of life.

Stuart Fleming, *The Egyptians.* New York: New Discovery, 1992. This book focuses on life in ancient Egypt and has a good deal of information about women.

Geraldine Harris and Delia Pemberton, *Illustrated Encyclopedia of Ancient Egypt.* New York: Peter Bedrick, 1999. This excellent book covers the entire period of ancient Egypt, its history, and its people.

Nathaniel Harris, *Everyday Life in Ancient Egypt.* New York: Franklin Watts, 1994. An insightful book about the ancient Egyptian way of life.

Viviane Koenig, *The Ancient Egyptians: Life in the Nile Valley.* Brookfield, CT: Millbrook, 1992. A book that describes the world and life of the ancient Egyptians.

Fiona MacDonald, *Ancient Egyptians.* New York: Barron's Education Series, 1992. The author focuses on various aspects of early Egyptian life.

———, *Women in Ancient Egypt.* New York: Peter Bedrick, 1999. This excellent book presents an overall look at the life of women in ancient Egypt.

Milton Meltzer, *In the Days of the Pharaoh.* New York: Franklin Watts, 2001. This book has a great deal of information about general life in Egypt as well as the status of women in that society.

Jacqueline Morley, *How Would You Survive as an Ancient Egyptian?* New York: Franklin Watts, 1995. The author describes the harsh life of the ancient Egyptians.

Neil Morris, *The Atlas of Ancient Egypt.* New York: Peter Bedrick, 2000. This book focuses on life in ancient Egypt.

Tom Streissguth, *Queen Cleopatra.* Minneapolis: Lerner, 2000. A fascinating look at this queen and leader of Egypt.

Web Sites

Daily Life in Ancient Egypt (http://members.aol.com/bkdonnclass/

Egyptlife.html). This excellent Web site contains material on various aspects of ancient Egyptian life and is written by members of a class of sixth graders in Glen Burnie, Maryland.

The Women of Ancient Egypt (www.expage.com/womenofegypt). This site offers glimpses of important women in Egyptian history, including Hatshepsut, Queen Tiy, and Queen Nefertiti.

Works Consulted

Books

Ancient Healing. Lincolnwood, IL: Publications International, 1997. This book has an excellent chapter on medicine and healing in ancient Egypt.

James Henry Breasted, *A History of Egypt.* Safety Harbor, FL: Simon, 2001. Originally published in 1909, this book is a history of Egypt through the eyes of an early–twentieth–century historian.

Bob Brier and Hoyt Hobbs, *Daily Life of the Ancient Egyptians.* Westport, CT: Greenwood, 1999. This book offers an insightful glimpse into the lives of the ancient Egyptians, including good coverage of the role of women.

Rosalie David, *Handbook of Life in Ancient Egypt.* New York: Facts On File, 1998. This excellent book offers a great deal of information about life in ancient Egypt. David is the author of over twenty books on Egypt.

Editors of Time–Life Books, *Ramses II: Magnificence on the Nile.* Alexandria, VA: Time–Life, 1993. A look at Egypt during the reign of this pharaoh. The book also includes information on Nefertari and the Egyptian way of life.

———, *What Life Was Like on the Bank of the Nile.* Alexandria, VA: Time–Life, 1997. An insightful look at the life of the ancient Egyptians.

Brian M. Fagan, *World Prehistory.* Upper Saddle River, NJ: Prentice Hall, 2002. An overview of ancient history with a good section on ancient Egypt.

Edith Flamarion, *Cleopatra: The Life and Death of a Pharaoh.* New York: Harry N. Abrams, 1997. This book presents an excellent biography of this Egyptian pharaoh and her life and times.

Joann Fletcher, *Ancient Egypt: Life, Myth, and Art.* New York: Barnes and Noble, 1999. This book offers an overall look at ancient Egypt and includes some excellent material on the role of women in that society.

Clare Gibson, *Goddess Symbols.* New York: Barnes and Noble, 1998. This book offers a look at various goddesses and has a good section on Isis and the role she played in ancient Egyptian life.

David E. Jones, *Women Warriors.* Washington, DC: Brassey's, 1997. A wide–ranging book about women throughout history and their leadership skills. The book includes a small section about ancient Egyptian women.

Reader's Digest, *Vanished Civilizations.* London: Reader's Digest, 2002. A comprehensive look at the ancient world, including a chapter on ancient Egypt.

John Romer, *Ancient Lives: Daily Life in Egypt of the Pharaohs.* New York: Holt, Rinehart, and Winston, 1998. The author and archaeologist focuses on a village near Thebes that has been excavated and describes the life of the workers and the families who once lived there.

David Silverman, *Ancient Egypt.* New York: Oxford University Press, 1997. This excellent book focuses on the history of ancient Egypt and has a very good chapter on Egyptian women.

Joyce Tyldesley, *Nefertiti: Egypt's Sun Queen.* New York: Viking, 1998. The author, a writer who specializes in Egyptian history and archaeology, offers an excellent biography of this queen and influential woman.

Evelyn Wells, *Hatshepsut.* New York: Doubleday, 1969. An excellent biography of this Egyptian queen and pharaoh.

Periodicals

Bob Edwards, "Egypt's Golden Empire," *Morning Edition*, National Public Radio, February 27, 2002.

Rick Gore, "Pharaohs of the Sun," *National Geographic*, April 2001.

———, "Ramses the Great," *National Geographic*, April 1991.

Zahi Hawass, "Egypt's Hidden Tombs Revealed," *National Geographic*, September 2001.

Betina Knapp, "The Archetypal Woman Fulfilled: Isis," *Symposium*, March 1, 1996.

Los Angeles Sentinel, "Our Heritage: Hatshepsut—the Greatest Female Ruler in History," April 7, 1999.

Paul Martin, "Ancient Egypt," *National Geographic Traveler*, March 1999.

Medical Post, "The First Healers: Women and Medicine in Ancient History," March 10, 1998.

Rumoko Rashidi, "The African Woman as Heroine," *Michigan Citizen*, September 28, 2002.

Kent R. Weeks, "Valley of the Kings," *National Geographic*, September 1998.

Internet Sources

Ancient Egypt: Medicine, "Ancient Egyptian Medicine," www.reshafine.org. il/ad/egupt/timelines/topics/medicine.htm.

Sameh M. Arab, "Medicine in Ancient Egypt," Arab World Books, www.arabworldbooks.com/articles8.htm.
David Bediz, "The Story of Hatshepsut," Portraits by Bulent Bediz, www.bediz.com/hatshep/story.html.
Casey Boone, "Ancient Egyptian Games," EMuseum, Minnesota State University, Mankato, www.mnsu.edu/emuseum/prehistory/egypt/dailylife/games.html.
Sarah Burns, "Ancient Egyptian Houses," EMuseum, Minnesota State University, Mankato, 2003. www.mnsu.edu/emuseum/prehistory/egypt/dailylife/housing.html.
Crystalinks, "Women in Ancient Egypt," www.crystalinks.com/egyptianwomen.html.
Cheryl Dawley, "Ancient Egyptian Beauty Aids," EMuseum, Minnesota State University, Mankato. www.mnsu.edu/emuseum/prehistory/egypt/dailylife/beautyaids.html.
Jimmy Dunn, "Egypt: The Wonderful Land of Punt," Tour Egypt, September 23, 2003. www.touregypt.net/featurestories/punt.htm.
Egypt State Information Service, "Stockbreeding and the Hunt," www.sis.gov.eg/pharo/html/huntfrm.htm.
EMuseum, Minnesota State University, Mankato, "Kinship and Marriage," www.mnsu.edu/emuseum/prehistory/egypt/dailylife/kinship_marriage.html.
———, "Medicine," www.mnsu.edu/emuseum/prehistory/egypt/dailylife/medicine.html.
Joann Fletcher, "From Warrior Women to Female Pharaoh," BBC History, July 1, 2004. www.bbc.co.uk/history/ancient/egyptians/women_03.shtml.
Petra Habiger, "Early History: Menstruation, Menstrual Hygiene, and Woman's Health in Ancient Egypt," Museum of Menstruation and Woman's Health, www.mum.org/germnt5.htm.
Joey Katzen, "Cleopatra, the Last Pharaoh," www.joeykatzen.com/writing/cleopatra.html.
Holly Laite, "Differences in Gender," EMuseum, Minnesota State University, Mankato, www.mnsu.edu/emuseum/prehistory/dailylife/genders/htm.
Mitch Oachs, "Ancient Egyptian Diet," EMuseum, Minnesota State University, Mankato, 2002. www.mnsu.edu/emuseum/prehistory/egypt/dailylife/diet_egypt.htm.
Ahmes L. Pahor, "Medicine and Surgery in Ancient Egypt," Centre for the History of Medicine, http://medweb. bham.ac.uk/histmed/pahor.html.

Marie Parsons, "Childbirth and Children in Ancient Egypt," Tour Egypt, www.touregypt.net/featurestories/mothers/htm.

Joseph Perkins, "Lives of Non–Royal Women," EMuseum, Minnesota State University, Mankato, 2002. www.mnsu.edu/emuseum/prehistory/egypt/dailylife/non–royal%20women.htm.

Pharaoh MaatKare Hatshepsut, Daughter of Amun Ra, "Women in Ancient Egypt," www.maatkare.com/women.html.

Pharaonic Egypt, "Ancient Egyptian Basketry," http://nefertiti.iwebland.com/basketry/index.html.

———, "Garments," http:/nefertiti.iwebland.com/timelines/topics/clothing.htm.

———, "Household Utensils and Materials," http://nefertiti.iwebland.com/utensils/index.html.

Geraldine Pinch, "Ancient Egyptian Magic," BBC, www.bbc.co.uk/history/ancient/egyptians/magic_01.shtml.

Caroline Seawright, "Hatshepsut, Female Pharaoh of Egypt," Tour Egypt, www.touregypt.net/historicalessays/hatshepsut.htm.

———, "Women in Ancient Egypt," Egypt Voyager, February 10, 2001. www.egyptvoyager.com/articles_womeninancientegypt_02.htm.

Ilene Springer, "Just What the Doctor Ordered in Ancient Egypt," *Tour Egypt Monthly,* www.touregypt.net/magazine/mag05012001/magf4.htm.

Kozue Takahashi, "Ancient Egyptian Hairstyles," EMuseum, Minnesota State University, Mankato. www.mnsu.edu/emuseum/prehistory/egypt/dailylife/hairstyles.html.

Alison Thiele, "Ancient Egyptian Midwifery and Childbirth, " EMuseum, Minnesota State University, Mankato, 2002. www.mnsu.edu/emuseum/prehistory/egypt/dailylife/midwifery.htm.

Index

Picture Credits

Cover image: Dahesh Museum of Art, New York, USA/Bridgeman Art Library
The Art Archive/Musée de Louvre Paris/Dagli Orti, 69
The Art Archive/Museum voor Schone Kunsten Ghent/Dagli Orti, 79
Ashmolean Museum, University of Oxford, UK/Bridgeman Art Library, 31
© Borromeo/Art Resource, NY, 22, 47
British Library, London, UK/Bridgeman Art Library, 82
© Corel Corporation, 45
Egyptian National Museum, Cairo, Egypt/Bridgeman Art Library, 28
© Giraudon/Art Resource, NY, 53, 74
Giraudon / Bridgeman Art Library, 11
© Hulton/Archive by Getty Images, 34, 89
© Charles & Josette Lenars/CORBIS, 19, 54, 94
© Erich Lessing/Art Resource, NY, 7, 29, 37, 48, 64, 76, 96
Mary Evans Picture Library, 77, 81
© Nimatallah/Art Resource, NY, 12
© Gianni Dagli Orti/CORBIS, 43, 86
© Scala/Art Resource, NY, 42, 73, 87
© Sandro Vannini/CORBIS, 91
© Werner Forman/Art Resource, NY, 16, 39
© Werner Forman/CORBIS, 57, 66
Whitford & Hughes, London, UK/Bridgeman Art Library, 97
Peter Willi/Bridgeman Art Library, 20
© Roger Wood/CORBIS, 33

About the Author

Anne Wallace Sharp is the author of one book of adult nonfiction, *Gifts*, a compilation of stories about hospice patients; and several children's books, including *Daring Women Pirates* and eight previous titles for Lucent Books. In addition, she has written numerous magazine articles for both the adult and children's market. A retired registered nurse, Sharp has a degree in history. Her other interests include reading, traveling, and spending time with her two grandchildren, Jacob and Nicole. Sharp lives in Beavercreek, Ohio.